Macmillan Computer Science Series

Consulting Editor
Professor F.H. Sumner, University of Manchest

continued overleaf

Tom Manns and Michael Coleman, *Software Quality Assurance*
Brian Meek, *Fortran, PL/1 and the Algols*
A Mével and T. Guéguen, *Smalltalk-80*
Barry Morrell and Peter Whittle, *CP/M 80 Programmer's Guide*
Y. Nishinuma and R. Espesser, *UNIX — First Contact*
Pim Oets, *MS-DOS and PC-DOS — A Practical Guide, second edition*
A.I. Pilavakis, *UNIX Workshop*
Christian Queinnec, *LISP*
E.J. Redfern, *Introduction to Pascal for Computational Mathematics*
Gordon Reece, *Microcomputer Modelling by Finite Differences*
W.P. Salman, O. Tisserand and B. Toulout, *FORTH*
L.E. Scales, *Introduction to Non-linear Optimization*
Peter S. Sell, *Expert Systems — A Practical Introduction*
A.G. Sutcliffe, *Human—Computer Interface Design*
Colin J. Theaker and Graham R. Brookes, *A Practical Course on Operating Systems*
M.R. Tolhurst et al., *Open Systems Interconnection*
J-M. Trio, *8086—8088 Architecture and Programming*
M.J. Usher, *Information Theory for Information Technologists*
B.S. Walker, *Understanding Microprocessors*
Colin Walls, *Programming Dedicated Microprocessors*
I.R. Wilson and A.M. Addyman, *A Practical Introduction to Pascal — with BS6192, second edition*

Non-series
Roy Anderson, *Management, Information Systems and Computers*
I.O. Angell, *Advanced Graphics with the IBM Personal Computer*
J.E. Bingham and G.W.P. Davies, *Planning for Data Communications*
B.V. Cordingley and D. Chamund, *Advanced BASIC Scientific Subroutines*
N. Frude, *A Guide to SPSS/PC+*
Barry Thomas, *A Postscript Cookbook*

Introduction to occam 2 on the Transputer

Graham R Brookes and
Andrew J Stewart

Department of Computer Science
University of Hull

MACMILLAN

First published 1989

Published by
MACMILLAN EDUCATION LTD
Houndsmills, Basingstoke, Hampshire RG21 2XS
and London
Companies and representatives
throughout the world

Laserset by
Ponting–Green Publishing Services, London
Printed and bound in Great Britain at
The Camelot Press Ltd, Southampton

British Library Cataloguing in Publication Data
Brookes, Graham R.
    Introduction to occam 2 on the Transputer.
    — (Macmillan computer science series).
    1. Computer systems. Programming languages.
    occam 2 language
    I. Title   II. Stewart, Andrew J.
    005.13'3
    ISBN 0–333–45340–9

Contents

Preface

Traditionally computer programming has been sequential in nature. There has been the need to write a program to follow an exact sequence of steps to attain the required result. As parallel computers become more common, and the operation of existing computers itself becomes more parallel, there is a need to have the ability to write parallel programs. This book provides an introduction to programming in one such parallel language, namely, occam 2. In the text it will become apparent that the nature of this language is such that writing a parallel program becomes easier to understand and write than to achieve the same operation in a sequential language.

Since occam 2 was intended to be the assembly language for use on the transputer which has been developed by Inmos Ltd, an overview of the operation of a transputer and its characteristic novel architecture is provided in Chapter 2. This illustrates many of the important features that the language uses to achieve parallelism. However, a detailed understanding of the material of that chapter is not essential to the rest of the text and the less discerning reader may omit the chapter. Central to the parallel programming is the concept of a program consisting of a series of processes, whose execution may be achieved in parallel. The communication and synchronisation between consistuent processes provide the framework on which the language is developed.

The contents of the book have been developed from courses of lectures given to undergraduates on concurrency. It aims to provide support for practical programming in concurrency using the language occam 2. No previous experience of writing parallel programs is assumed, but a general knowledge of programming techniques is beneficial.

Several practical examples are developed throughout the text to illustrate a few of the wide range of suitable applications for parallel programming techniques. A bibliography is provided where the reader may consult in more depth some aspects of the language.

The authors wish to acknowledge the assistance and encouragement of colleagues. In particular we thank several from the Department of Computer Science at the University of Sheffield for discussions in the early stages of the preparation of this text.

1 Introduction

The development of computer applications has always depended to a large extent on the speed of the processor units available. Since the construction of the first electronic computers, the speed of operation has increased by approximately a factor of ten each decade. This improvement in performance over recent decades is shown in figure 1.1. By and large this improvement in performance has been achieved by making the individual components work faster. These developments are becoming increasingly expensive and difficult as technology begins to be constrained by fundamental physical limitations such as the velocity of light. New improvements in present generations of integrated circuits are likely to provide smaller returns, in terms of increased speed.

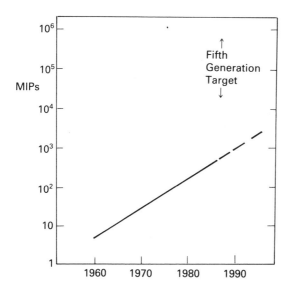

Figure 1.1 Development of conventional computer systems

The demand for computing power shows no signs of abating as people in all areas of technology enhance their understanding by more detailed analysis methods. Typical present computer applications use processor speeds of 1–10 million instructions per second (MIPs). In the future VLSI offers the potential of much greater circuit complexity, but without sustaining the necessary increases in circuit performance. The sort of processing power that is needed to satisfy 'fifth generation software' will need processor speeds in the region of 10 000–1 000 000 MIPs. A number of techniques have been tried to provide this increased performance, and future developments will undoubtedly lead to some increase in the speed of conventional processors; nevertheless a single processor will still not be able to provide the processing speed required.

The traditional perspective of machines based on the von Neumann architecture has been founded on the concept that processing is expensive in comparison to memory. A typical von Neumann computer architecture consists of one processor and one memory area. Both data and instructions are stored in this memory area and so the processor needs almost constant access. A program counter keeps the address of the next instruction and this is updated as the program is executed. Such machines execute single instructions on single data items and are referred to as SISD machines (Single Instruction, Single Data). This has led to the so-called 'von Neumann bottleneck'. An obvious strategy for improving the performance is to introduce some measure of parallelism in the process by the provision of additional processors. An idealistic parallel computer is one in which each processor has access to shared global memory. However, adding an additional processor to the system does not necessarily double the processing power. The introduction of two processors which share the same memory for communications purposes means they must use memory on a bus. There is thus a processor–memory bottleneck, and the expected gain in performance is not achieved. Such a bottleneck is illustrated in figure 1.2 where there are four processors accessing four areas of the memory space. This leads to problems of contention; for example, if both processors need to access the same memory location at exactly the same time then some sort of system must exist to decide which processor gets access to the memory and which processor has to wait until the other has finished. Such a scheme of arbitration for two processors can exist without any significant loss in processing power. The addition of further processors makes the problems of arbitration more difficult, and increases in performance are not linearly related to the number of processors.

An important trend at present is the production of parallel processors at a relatively low cost. Parallel processing machines, referred to as MIMD (Multiple Instruction, Multiple Data) machines, have existed since the early 1950s when the Univac 1 was introduced. Parallel processing can exist in a computer in a variety of ways, for instance in the use of pipelining, array

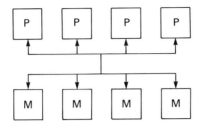

Figure 1.2 Diagram illustrating von Neumann bottleneck

processors, functional units and multiprocessors. The concept of a pipeline can be regarded as a series of processing elements connected into a 'pipe', through which data is allowed to flow. The processing elements are arranged in such a way that each successive element performs the next stage of the program. This allows a measure of parallel processing whilst retaining a simple data flow and controlled use of communications. Pipelining, in its simplest form, is a situation where the 'fetch' instruction and the 'execute' instruction operate in parallel. The Cray machine, for example, uses the pipelining technique, and pipelining is commonly seen in bit-slice designs and microcoded systems.

- In array processing several processors execute the same instruction but on different data originating from the memory associated with each processor – these are usually referred to as SIMD machines (Single Instruction, Multiple Data).
- Functional parallelism allows several functional units such as adder, boolean logic, and multiplier to operate simultaneously on different data.
- Multiprocessing allows several processors, each executing its own instruction stream but operating on data which may be shared between all processors.

Multiprocessing sounds attractive and is used, for example, in the Cray XMP48. Difficulties can arise in that if the right topology is not used for the interconnection of the processors then the net result of parallel processing may be to slow the response down. However, multiprocessing on a large scale is now a distinct possibility since the increased functionality given by increasing the number of components on a single chip has not yet been exhausted.

In spite of the attractive benefits of parallel processing in terms of increased performance, there are major problems relating to communication, synchronisation and the scheduling of the work between the different processors. Communication is concerned with getting the correct data to the processors at the correct time for their efficient use. The processors need to communicate with each other and hence share a common bus. As the number of processors increases, the system quickly reaches the state where a processor spends most of its time waiting to use the bus. The problem of dividing a program between several processors is complex, and typically a situation exists where processors finish their tasks at different times and may be left idle waiting for other processors to complete their tasks. Problems of sychronisation can occur with the processor which is dedicated to controlling the other processors and detecting when the other processors have finished their tasks. In order to overcome these problems many scheduling algorithms have been developed to try and improve performance.

One development in the parallel processing area is provided by a new computer architecture developed by Inmos Ltd as a microprocessor. This new processor is called a transputer (TRANSistor comPUTER) and includes not only processor and memory components, but also a channel, or **LINK**, for communicating with other transputers and to other devices. This link and its properties comprise one of the fundamental distinguishing features of this novel architecture. Communication across the link takes place only once both ends are ready, so that events are synchronised. The synchronisation of events was one of the major problems in early attempts at parallel processing. For each transputer there are four such links, which means that they can be interconnected in a wide range of different configurations, and are therefore very well suited to multiprocessor systems. The basic transputer processor speed is in the region of 10 MIPs, but because transputers do not share the same communication bus the overall processing power increases linearly with the number of transputers added; an array of, say, 100 such transputers should provide a speed in the region of 1000 MIPs. In the case of conventional processors the overall processing power improvement starts to diminish with the involvement of around six processors.

The transputer architecture uses processes as the fundamental standard software building block, and it provides a direct implementation of a process in hardware. A process is an independent computation which can communicate with other processes being executed at the same time. Communication between processes running on transputers is achieved by using explicitly defined channels. A process can itself consist of a number of sub-processes and the transputer can implement these sub-processes by time-sharing, with special instructions being provided to support communication. Processes and an example of their interconnection are shown in figure 1.3.
The transputer provides a number of links to support point-to-point communications between transputers, thereby enabling processes to be distributed over a network of transputers. It is thus possible to program systems containing multiple interconnected transputers in which each transputer

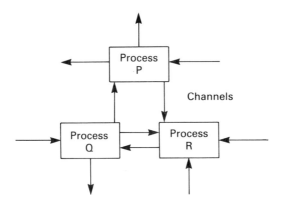

Figure 1.3 Processes connected together by channels

implements a set of processes. It should also be noted that the transputer can only send a message directly to another one to which it is physically wired. The ability to specify a hardwired function as an occam process provides the architectural framework for transputers with specialised functions such as graphics.

Whilst the transputer can be programmed in most high-level languages, benefit can be gained from the architecture if the system is programmed in the concurrent language occam. Named after the philosopher William of Occam, this has evolved as the native language of the transputer. A system can be completely designed and programmed in occam from the system configuration down to the low-level input–output and real-time interrupts. occam allows concurrency to be explicitly defined within the program. An important feature of both occam and the transputer is that a program written in occam targeted for a system of several transputers will, with a few program modifications, also execute on a one-transputer system, although more slowly. How a program which consists of three processes, P, Q and R, might run on a single transputer, and how the same three processes run on three transputers, is illustrated in figure 1.4.

Briefly, some of the features of the programming language occam are the following. The assignment statement, which is actually a primitive process, is similar to that of conventional languages except that explicit parenthesisation is required. Input and output are facilitated through the use of channels, for example

```
InputChannel ? char
```

would input a character char via the channel called InputChannel, and

```
OutputChannel ! char
```

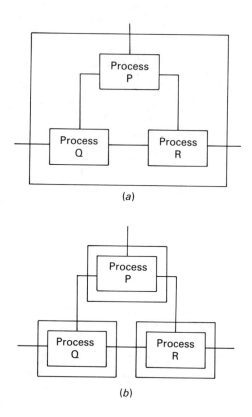

(a)

(b)

Figure 1.4 A program running either on a single transputer (a) or on a network of three transputers (b)

would output a character char via the channel OutputChannel. Program flow may be handled with **IF** and **WHILE** constructs. In conventional notations, statements lexically following one another are executed in sequence. In occam, statements are replaced by processes which operate in sequence or concurrently, depending on whether they are preceded by the **SEQ** or the **PAR** construct respectively. Concurrent processes are mutually synchronised and communicate with each other via occam channels, and the external links are implemented, programmatically, as channels. The occam **ALT** construct provides a mechanism whereby a process can proceed upon receipt of the first available input from any of a number of alternative concurrent processes. Finally, timer interrupts and external event interrupts are consistently handled as channels, as though they constitute input from other concurrent processes.

Although occam is not an assembly language, the architecture of the transputer so closely implements occam's constructs, and occam so completely provides for the control of the hardware, that no assembler is required or desired for virtually any application. With the exception of its unique constructs for expressing parallelism and interprocess communication, the expressions and flow control constructs in occam are similar to those of more common notations.

The range of applications suitable for the use of transputers is very wide. When faced with large and complex problems, the natural tendency is to divide the problem into smaller ones which can be solved in parallel; this is obviously well suited to the use of transputers. In large and complex computational problems, such an approach is often referred to as 'divide and conquer'. Successive use of the divide and conquer principle creates an evaluation tree for solving the problem in parallel. There are many ways of processing the tree itself.

The operation of a graphics workstation provides a good illustration. The stages of its operation can be divided into areas such as conversion, translation, rotation or projection, windowing, sorting, hidden surfaces, and display. All of these areas can be regarded as processes which are suitable for subdivision and subsequent parallel processing.

Chapter 2 provides a description of the transputer and its basic architecture. There are several items in the transputer range of products, so the description is general rather than related to a specific configuration. Chapter 2 provides an overview of the operation of the transputer, but a full understanding of the material of that chapter is not essential for the understanding of occam 2. The reader may prefer to omit this chapter.

Chapter 3 outlines the notation of occam 2, and Chapter 4 considers the data types available within the language. Having established the framework of the language, in Chapter 5 we then consider the constructs provided within occam 2. Several examples are given to illustrate the main constructs. In Chapter 6 arithmetic expressions are described; finally, functions and procedures are considered in Chapter 7.

Throughout the book where reference is made to occam this is taken to refer to the current version, namely occam 2. Some additional features are being added in the development of the language.

2 The transputer

2.1 System design

The transputer is a high-performance microprocessor uniquely designed to facilitate interprocess and interprocessor communication. The language-directed architecture explicitly supports communicating sequential processes through use of the programming language occam. The transputer has special hardware facilities for process scheduling, interprocess channel communication, interprocessor external serial link communications, and timer and external interrupts. These facilities are all implemented in a consistent manner, their management being expressed within the context of the occam language. The transputer architecture defines a family of programmable VLSI components, which includes the T212, T414 and a floating-point processor T800. The general features of the transputer architecture are shown in the block diagram figure 2.1. The architecture consists of the following features:

- Fast Reduced Instruction Set Computer (RISC) processor
- Fast on-chip static Random Access Memory (RAM)
- External memory controller
- Hardware time-slicing features
- High-speed serial links (Inmos links) – four in the case of the T414.

Some of the comparative features of the T212, T414 and T800 are given in table 2.1.

The T414, as a member of the family of transputers, will be used to illustrate features of the transputer architecture; it provides users with 10 MIPs processing power with memory and communications capability, all on a single CMOS chip.

2.2 System architecture

The T414 transputer integrates a 32-bit microprocessor and has 2 Kbytes of high-speed (50 ns) on-chip RAM and 4 Gbytes of linear address space with a 25 Mbyte/s memory interface. The four links (Inmos links) on each T414 provide point-to-point communication with full duplex DMA transfer and are capable of transfer rates up to 20 Mbits/s. A block diagram of the T414 is given in figure 2.2.

Table 2.1 Comparative features of T212, T414 and T800

	T212	T414	T800
Internal register and bus width	16-bit	32-bit	32-bit
External memory interface width	8/16-bit	32-bit	32-bit
50 ns on-chip RAM	2 kbyte	2 kbyte	4 kbyte
Linearly addressable memory space	64 kbyte	4 Gbyte	4 Gbyte
Minimum number of processor cycles for external RAM access	2	3	3
Performance	10 MIPs	10 MIPs	10 MIPs
Serial links (5, 10 or 20 Mbits/s)	4	4	4
Process scheduling in hardware with submicrosecond context switch	Yes	Yes	Yes
Internal timers for real-time processing	Yes	Yes	Yes
External event interrupt with submicro- second typical interrupt latency	Yes	Yes	Yes
On-chip 64-bit floating point coprocessor (ANSI IEEE 754-1985)	No	No	Yes
1.5 MFLOPs sustainable	–	–	Yes
High-performance graphics support	No	No	Yes

The internal memory, 2 Kbytes for the T414, provides a maximum data rate of 80 Mbytes/s compared with about 25 Mbytes/s for external memory. From the programmer's point of view there is no visible difference between the two. Any internal RAM is mapped onto the bottom-most part of the address space, and if the address for a memory access lies within this range then internal RAM is accessed, otherwise the external data/address bus is activated. The provision of internal RAM has two advantages. Firstly, critical sections of code and data can be located there, resulting in a significant increase in program execution speed. Secondly, it enables transputers to be used without any external memory provided that the program and data are not too large, thereby resulting in large savings in physical space.

The T414 can directly access a linear address space of 4 Gbytes. The memory interface uses a 32-bit wide address/data bus and provides data at a rate up to 25 Mbytes/s. The bus width does not have to match the 32 bits of the processor: any multiple of 8 bits would be acceptable. The address space of the T414 is signed and byte addressed. Addresses in the range [#80000000 FOR #800] reference on-chip memory. Words are aligned along 4-byte boundaries. The first 18 word locations of the address space are used for system purposes. The next available location is then referred to as

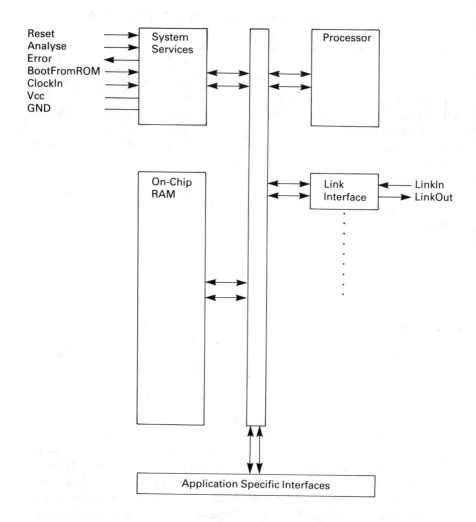

Figure 2.1   Block diagram of a transputer

MemStart. A suitable definition for MemStart for incorporation into an occam program is:

```
VAL MemStart IS #80000048:
```

The top of the address space is used for ROM-based code. If the transputer is configured to bootstrap from ROM then the processor commences execution from address #7FFFFFFE. If the transputer is configured to use an externally defined memory interface configuration then this is stored at locations #7FFFFF6C to #7FFFFFF8.

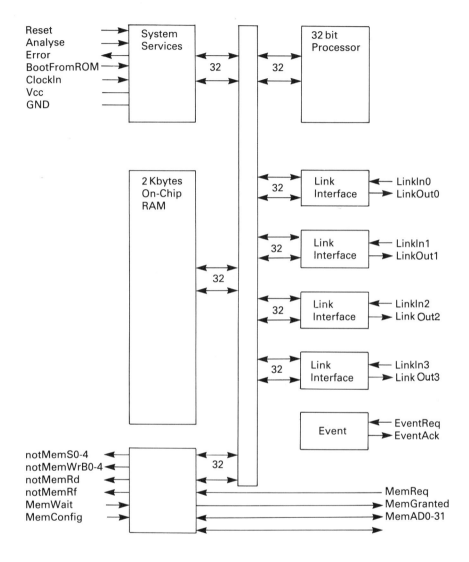

Figure 2.2   Block diagram of the T414 transputer

A configurable memory controller provides all the timing and control signals as well as supporting memory-mapped peripherals. This controller may be configured to suit a range of memory systems. One of the 14 preset configurations may be used, or an alternative may be supplied externally. The T414 memory interface cycle has six states referred to as T-states. The duration of each T-state is configured to suit the memory used, and has a duration between one and four times the value of Tm, where Tm is half the processor cycle time. However, the duration of the T-state T4 may be extended by wait states. The T-states are as follows:

T1   address setup time before address valid strobe
T2   address hold time after address valid strobe
T3   read cycle tristate/write cycle data setup
T4   extended for wait states
T5   read or write data
T6   end tristate/data hold

Communications to the transputer are provided by the standard Inmos links. These links may be interfaced to the peripherals via an Inmos link adapter whereby the peripheral may signal to the T414 via the EventReq pin with which the T414 handshakes using EventAck. The T414 implements a hardware channel to allow low to high transitions on the EventReq pin to be communicated to a process as a sychronising message. An occam channel may be associated with the EventReq pin by a channel association. The conventional name and the value used for this channel are:

```
PLACE Event AT #80000020:
```

Event behaves like an ordinary channel, and a process may synchronise with a low to high transition on the EventReq pin by using the occam construct

```
Event ? signal
```

The process waits until the channel Event is ready, the channel being made ready by the low to high transition on the EventReq pin. When the process is able to proceed, and if it executes at high priority, then it will take priority over any low-priority process which may be executing when the transition occurs on the EventReq pin.

High-level language execution is made secure with, for example, array bound checking and arithmetic overflow detection. If the compiler is unable to check that a given construct contains only valid expressions and processes, then extra instructions are compiled in order to perform the necessary check at runtime. If the result of this check indicates that an error has occurred then the processor's Error flag is set. This error can be handled either internally by software or externally by sensing the Error pin. If the processor has been halted as a result of an error, then the links continue with any outstanding transfers, the memory continues to provide refresh cycles and the transputer may be analysed. When a high-priority process preempts a low-priority process the current value of the Error flag is preserved and the Error flag is reset. When there are no high-priority processes to run, then the current state of the Error flag is lost and the preserved state is restored as part of commencing to execute the preempted low-priority process.

Timing in occam is provided by use of a timer channel which can only provide input. The value input from the timer is the current time, which is represented as an integer value. The cycle of the clock depends on the wordsize, on the amount by which the reading is incremented at each tick, and on the frequency of the clock ticks. Each of these will depend on the particular implementation on the hardware on which occam is running. In the case of the transputer the ticks are in units of (input clock rate)/(5*64) which normally works out at 64 μs per tick. With a 64 μs tick and a 16-bit integer, then the cycle time would be approximately 4.2 s; with a 32-bit integer the corresponding cycle time would be approximately 76 hours.

The processor has timers to support two levels of priority. The priority 1 (low-priority) processes are executed whenever there are no active priority 0 (high-priority) processes. High-priority processes are expected to execute for short time intervals. If one or more such processes can proceed then one is selected and allowed to execute until it has to wait for a communication, a timer input, or until the process is completed. However, if no high-priority process is able to proceed and one or more low-priority processes is able to proceed, then one of the low-priority processes is selected. Low-priority processes are time-sliced to provide an even distribution of processor time between computationally intensive tasks. If there are n low-priority processes, then the maximum latency, expressed as the time from when a low-priority process becomes active to the time at which it starts processing, is $2n - 2$ time-slice periods. Each time-slice period is 4096 cycles, which is about 800 μs. In order to ensure that low-priority processes do proceed, high-priority processes must not continuously occupy the processor for a period equal to that of a time-slice. If a low-priority process is waiting for an external channel to become ready, and there are no active high-priority processes, then the interrupt latency, which is the time interval from when the channel becomes ready until the process starts executing, is typically 12 processor cycles, though it may extend to a maximum of 58 cycles.

The system services comprise the clocks, power and initialisation used by the whole of the transputer. The Reset and Analyse inputs enable the T414 to be initialised or halted in a way which preserves its state for subsequent analysis. Whilst the T414 is running, both Reset and Analyse are held low. The T414 is initialised by pulsing Reset high whilst holding Analyse low. Operation ceases immediately and all current state information is lost. When Reset goes low the transputer sets up the memory interface configuration as appropriate. The processor and links start operating after the memory interface configuration cycle is complete and sufficient refresh cycles have been executed to initialise any dynamic RAM. The processor then bootstraps. When initialising after power-on, a time is specified during which the 5V supply, V_{cc}, must be within specification. Reset must be high, and the input on ClockIn must be oscillating. Reset is taken low after the specified time has elapsed. In order to analyse a system following a Reset, the first step is for the Analyse to be taken high. This causes the T414 to halt within three time-slice periods, approximately 3 μs, plus the time for any priority process to stop processing. Any outputting links continue to operate until they complete the remainder of the current word. Input links continue to receive data. Provided that there are no delays in sending acknowledgements, the links in the system will therefore cease activity within a few microseconds. Sufficient time must be allowed both for the processor to halt and for all link traffic to be completed before Reset is asserted. The memory interface is not affected by Analyse, or Reset, while Analyse is held high. If refresh cycles are enabled it continues to refresh external dynamic RAM.

2.3 Inmos links

The transputer architecture provides point-to-point communications by way of links called Inmos links. In the case of the T414 there are four such links. Each link provides two occam channels, one in each direction. The communication via any link may occur concurrently with communication on all other links and with program execution. Synchronisation of processes at each end of a link is automatic and requires no explicit programming. The T414 links implement the standard intertransputer communications. The conventional names and values for the channels are:

```
PLACE Link0Output AT #80000000:
PLACE Link1Output AT #80000004:
PLACE Link2Output AT #80000008:
PLACE Link3Output AT #8000000C:
PLACE Link0Input AT #80000010:
PLACE Link1Input AT #80000014:
PLACE Link2Input AT #80000018:
PLACE Link3Input AT #8000001C:
```

The links are connected by wiring a LinkOut to a LinkIn, and this is illustrated in figure 2.3.

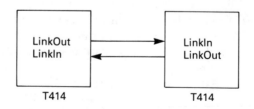

Figure 2.3 Transputer link connection

Each link consists of a serial input and a serial output, both of which are used to carry data and link control information. The link protocol is reminiscent of the serial ASCII protocol used with RS232, but differs in that an acknowledgement is returned following each transmitted byte of data, thereby facilitating synchronised communication between concurrent processes. A message is transmitted as a sequence of data packets. Each data packet is transmitted as a one bit followed by a further one bit, followed by eight data bits followed by a zero bit. After transmitting a data packet the sender transputer waits until an acknowledge is received which signifies that the receiving transputer is ready to receive another byte. The acknowledge consists of a one bit followed by a zero bit. The link protocol format is shown in figure 2.4.

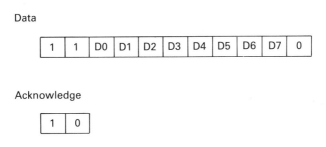

Figure 2.4 Link protocol format

Data and acknowledge packets are time-multiplexed down each signal line, with a pair of lines providing two occam channels, one in each direction. The receiving transputer can send an acknowledge as soon as the data packet has been identified, so transmission can be continuous, provided there is sufficient buffer space for another data packet and the inputting process is ready to receive the previous data packet. This protocol synchronises the communication of each byte of data, providing reliable communications even between transputers of inherently different speeds. The communications protocol is independent of word length, so transputers using different word lengths can communicate directly.

The link connections allow some selection of the link speeds. When the Link0Special and Link123Special inputs are held low the communications rate on all four links is twice the input clock frequency. Since the standard ClockIn frequency is 5 MHz, this means that the standard communications rate is 10 Mbits/s, which is more than 500 times faster than RS232. If Link123Special is held high then Link1, Link2 and Link3 all operate at the ClockIn frequency.

The provision of links allows intertransputer communications, and hence the connection of transputers into arrays. A wide variety of configurations are possible, partly dependent on the number of links used. Figure 2.5 shows a subset of a number of alternatives; the choice appropriate to any given case is influenced by the nature of the requirements. For example, all four links may be used to interconnect a pair of transputers, and these can then act as a node in a three-dimensional lattice pattern.

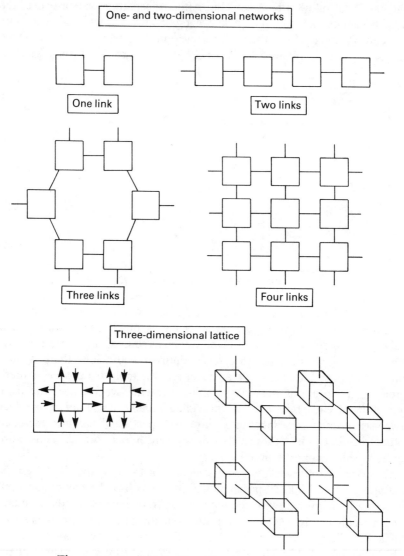

Figure 2.5 Examples of intertransputer connections

3 occam notation

3.1 Channels and concurrency

Processes in occam provide the fundamental building blocks for the language, and the transputer provides the direct implementation of a process. In occam, processes which are independent computations can communicate with other processes at the same time to form concurrent systems. Each process may be regarded as a 'black box' with some particular internal state. These separate processes can communicate with each other by way of point-to-point communication channels. The processes are finite in that each process starts, performs a number of actions and then terminates or stops. The action that each process performs may be either a set of sequential processes as in a conventional language, or a set of parallel processes.

Each process may itself consist of other processes, each of which can execute either sequentially or in parallel. Thus in occam the concept of processes means there is an amount of inherent internal concurrency in the language. The degree of concurrency which is achieved at any given time will alter as processes start and terminate.

A pair of communicating processes communicate using a one-way channel, an occam channel, which connects the two processes. Each channel therefore provides a one-way connection between two concurrent processes; one process outputs a message to the channel and the other process inputs the message from the channel. The important concept with the channels is that the communications are synchronised and unbuffered. If a channel is used for input for one process and the same channel is used for output from another process, then communications can take place only when both processes are ready. Once both processes are ready then the inputting and outputting processes proceed. The value to be output is copied from the outputting process to the inputting process. This communication is equivalent to handshaking in other hardware systems. If an input process is reached before the corresponding output process on that channel is reached then the input will wait until the output becomes ready. Should the output be ready first then it will wait for the corresponding input to be ready on that channel.

A process may be ready to communicate on any one of a number of channels. Communication takes place when another process is ready to communicate on one of the channels. Since a process may have internal concurrency, it may have many input channels and output channels performing communications at the same time.

Since the transputer implements the occam concepts of concurrency and communication, occam can be used to program both single transputers and a network of transputers. In the case of a single transputer, it shares its time between concurrent processes and channel communication. In this case, the communication is via memory-to-memory data transfer. For a network of transputers, each transputer executes the process which has been allocated to it. The communication between occam processes on different transputers is via occam links. The same occam process can thus be implemented on either a single transputer or on a network of transputers. The implementation using a network will achieve a better performance with regard to speed than the equivalent process on a single transputer. However, the cost and other overheads of such a network may be significant. The configuration chosen for any particular case is therefore dependent on considerations such as performance and cost.

3.2 Notation

In this book the notation used in the description of occam follows that adopted in the language definition by David May as described in Inmos (1984).

occam programs are built up from processes. The simplest process in an occam program is an action. An action can be composed of any of the following:

- assignment
- input
- output

where an assignment computes the value of an expression and sets a variable to this value which can be expressed as

```
assignment = variable := expression
```

This assignment is made provided the type of the variable is that of the expression, otherwise the assignment is invalid. Here the symbol := indicates the assignment. For example,

```
b := e
```

sets the value of the variable *b* to the value of the expression *e* and then terminates. Thus

```
y := 0
```

sets the value of y to zero.

A multiple assignment is also possible:

```
a, b, c := p + 3, q - 2, r
```

Here, for example, the assignment assigns the values of $p + 3$, $q - 2$, and r to the variables a, b, c respectively. In such multiple assignments, the values of the expressions to be assigned, i.e. $p + 3$, $q - 2$, and r in this case, are calculated and the actual assignments are then made in parallel. An interesting example is

```
a, b := b, a
```

where this has the effect of swapping the values of the variables a and b.

The meaning of

```
action = assignment | input | output
```

reflects the fact that a process may be either an assignment, an input or an output.

The written structure of an occam program is specified by the syntax. Each program statement occupies a single line, except that long statements can be broken over more than one line, as discussed shortly. Unlike some programming languages where the level of indentation is not obligatory, in occam the indentation of the lines of the program forms an intrinsic part of the syntax of the language. The syntax for the language construct sequence, **SEQ**, is discussed in detail in the next section, but it takes the form

```
sequence = SEQ
            {process}
```

This syntax denotes a sequence followed by one or more processes, each on a separate line and all indented by the same amount – two spaces beyond the **SEQ**. The notation {process} signifies the number of times that the syntactic object will occur; in this case the object is a process. The process will occur zero or more times. An extension to this notation would be

```
{0, expression} meaning a list of zero or more
                expressions, separated by commas
{1, expression} meaning a list of one or more
                expressions, separated by commas.
```

Long statements which require additional lines may have to be broken. When a statement is broken, the continuation of the statement on the following line must be indented at least as much as the first line of the statement. To break such a long statement, the break must be made immediately after any of the following:

- an assignment   : =
- a comma   ,
- a keyword   **IS, FROM** or **FOR**
- an operator   +, −, *, /, etc.
- a semicolon   ;

A text string may also be broken to continue on additional lines, but in this case the first line of the string ends with a '*' and the continuation on the following lines also starts with '*'.

A comment is preceded by the character pair '- -', and extends to the end of the line. Comments may not be indented less than the following statement.

```
SEQ -- A sequence
   -- An illustration of the use of comments
   -- A comment may not be indented less
   -- than the following statement
   ...
SEQ -- Another sequence
   ...
```

However in the following, the use of comments is invalid:

```
SEQ -- A sequence
-- An invalid comment, insufficient indentation
   ...
SEQ -- Another sequence
```

Input and output are used for communicating between processes. Input is indicated by the symbol ? . For example,

```
keyboard ? char
```

inputs the value from the channel keyboard and assigns it to the variable char and then the process terminates.

Output is indicated by the symbol ! . For example,

```
screen ! char
```

outputs the value of the variable char to the channel screen and then terminates.

4 Data types

Occam requires that every object that is used in the program must be declared before it can be used; this tells occam what sort of object it is dealing with. So far we have introduced the ideas of channels, using names such as keyboard and screen, and the use of variables, using names such as char without detailed specification of the relevant types.

First of all, objects in occam can be as long as the user wishes, but they must start with a letter of the alphabet. After the first letter, the rest of the name may be either a letter of the alphabet, or numbers or the dot character. Occam treats upper-case and lower-case characters as different, so that Counter and counter would represent different variables. Occam has a number of reserved words which cannot be used for variables, and these are written in upper case. The reserved words are given in table 4.1.

Table 4.1 Reserved words in occam

AFTER	IS	PROTOCOL
ALT	INT	REAL32
AND	INT16	REAL64
ANY	INT32	REM
AT	INT64	RESULT
BITAND	MINUS	RETYPES
BITNOT	MOSTNEG	ROUND
BITOR	MOSTPOS	SEQ
BOOL	NOT	SIZE
BYTE	OR	SKIP
CASE	PAR	STOP
CHAN OF	PLACE	TIMER
ELSE	PLACED	TIMES
FALSE	PLUS	TRUE
FOR	PORT OF	TRUNC
FROM	PRI	VAL
FUNCTION	PROC	VALOF
IF	PROCESSOR	WHILE

4.1 Primitive types

In occam every variable, expression and value has a type, which may be a primitive, array or record type. The type defines the length and interpretations of the type. The general representation of primitive types is given by:

```
type             = primitive.type | array.type

primitive.type   = CHAN OF protocol
                 | TIMER
                 | BOOL
                 | BYTE
                 | INT
                 | INT16
                 | INT32
                 | INT64
                 | REAL32
                 | REAL64
array.type       = [expression]type
```

So the following are the primitive types which are present in all implementations of occam:

- **CHAN OF** type   Each communication channel enables values of the specified type to be communicated between two concurrent processes.
- **TIMER**   Each timer provides a clock which can be used by any number of concurrent processes.
- **INT**   INT is the type of signed integer represented in twos complement form, supporting the following ranges of values n:
  - **INT16** $-32768 <= n < 32768$
  - **INT32** $-2147483648 <= n < 2147483648$
  - **INT64** $-2**63 <= n < 2**63$
- **REAL32**   Floating-point numbers using a sign bit, s, an 8-bit exponent, e, and 23-bit mantissa, f. The value of the number is positive if $s = 0$, negative if $s = 1$; its magnitude is:
  - $(2**(e-127))*1.f$ if $0 < e < 255$
  - $(2**-126)*0.f$ if $e = 0$ and $f <> 0$
  - 0 if $e = 0$ and $f = 0$
- **REAL64**   Floating-point numbers using a sign bit, s, an 11-bit exponent, e, and 52-bit mantissa, f. The value of the number is positive if $s = 0$, negative if $s = 1$; its magnitude is:
  - $(2**(e-1023))*1.f$ if $0 < e < 2047$
  - $(2**-1022)*0.f$ if $e = 0$ and $f <> 0$
  - 0 if $e = 0$ and $f = 0$
- **BOOL**   The values of type **BOOL** are **TRUE** and **FALSE**.

- **BYTE** The values of type **BYTE** are non-negative numbers less than 256.

A variable, expression or value may be declared to be one of the above types by use of a declaration of the form

```
declaration    = type name :
```

Note the use of : to signify the end of the declaration.

Variables of integer type would be specified as, for example,

```
INT x :
P
```

declares x as an integer to be used in the process P.

As described above, data types may be specified in various forms, but by way of illustration, variables of type integer can be given as:

```
INT    signal, counter :
```

Several variables, such as signal and counter in the above, can be specified at once provided each is separated by a comma. The type declaration is terminated by a colon as shown above. This colon joins the type specification to the process which follows it, and they are indented to the same level as the process that follows. The process which follows the specification is the one throughout which the specification is valid, and is usually referred to as the scope of the specification. This means that the same name may be used for different objects with different scopes. However, if there is a need for a variable to keep its value from one process to another then it is necessary to be sure that the variable is specified within the outer scope in a process which itself contains the inner process in which the variable is to be accessed.

As an illustration of a process which uses the type declaration **INT**, the following process is a non-terminating one which filters negative numbers from a sequence.

```
INT val:
WHILE TRUE
  SEQ
    c.1 ? val
    IF
      val >= 0
        c.2 ! val
      val < 0
        SKIP
```

Here values, called val, are read in as integers on the input channel c.1. If the value is zero or positive then the value is output on channel c.2; otherwise, if the value is negative, no corresponding value is output.

Communication between the component processes of a **PAR** construct must only be achieved using channels. occam does not allow values to be passed between processes using the option of shared variables. The reasoning behind this restriction is evident when we remember that for the **PAR** construct the processes which are running in parallel are executing in their own time, being synchronised only at times when they are communicating with each other by means of channels between them. It would be quite impossible to allow use of shared variables within such a framework. For example, if it were possible in occam to write:

```
INT v.1:
PAR
  p.1
  p.2
```

how would access to v.1 be controlled? Bear in mind that the number of physical processors needed to run a set of parallel processes is not defined in occam. In the example above, the processes p.1 and p.2 could be executing on the processor, or they could be executing on entirely separate processors – each processor having its own distinct memory area. One of the important aspects of occam is the facility to write parallel programs which behave correctly regardless of the mapping from processes to processors. If occam permitted us to write programs like the example above it would be extremely difficult to guarantee correctness.

Specification of a variable in occam does not initialise the value of that type to any particular value. The value of the variable can have any value until it is assigned or input within the process within which it has been specified. Once outside the process associated with its specification, the variable does not exist, and its value from within the process has no meaning once that process has terminated. For example, if we write

```
INT v.1, v.2:
SEQ
  process
```

the values of v.1 and v.2 are undefined until they are assigned to in some way – using either an assignment process or an input process. If v.1 or v.2 are used before they have been assigned to, the results will be unpredictable (and almost certainly wrong). So,

```
INT v.1, v.2, v.3:    -- values of v.1 and  v.2 undefined
SEQ
  v.3 := v.1 + v.2        -- wrong!
  v.1 := 0
  v.2 := 0                -- v.1 and v.2 now defined
```

When using arithmetic operators in occam with real operands the results of those operations are rounded to produce a value which is of the same type as their operands. In explicit type conversions rounding also occurs as well as in converting real literals. Truncation takes place only in explicit type conversions. In the case of rounding it is valid to round a real value to a value of type T provided that the real value differs from some other value of type T by at most one half in the least significant bit position of this new value. The result is the value of type T nearest to the original real value; if, however, two values of type T are equally near then the one in which the least significant bit is zero is chosen. In the case of truncation, it is also valid to truncate a real value to a value of type T provided that this real value differs from some other real value of type T by less than one in the least significant bit position. The result is the value of type T nearest to and not larger in magnitude than the original real value.

4.1.1 Channel types

Channels are all of type **CHAN OF** protocol. It is necessary to specify the data type and structure with which they are associated, and this is referred to as the protocol of the channel. A simple example of a channel which can carry integer values would be specified as

```
CHAN OF INT count :
```

Here the specification of **INT** defines the type of data that is to be communicated through the channel specified by count. If attempts to communicate data other than that of type **INT** via this channel are made an error will result. The specification thus gives the type for channel count as **CHAN OF INT**. For example,

```
CHAN OF INT c.1, c.2:
CHAN OF BOOL c.3:

INT v.1, v.2:
BOOL b.1:

SEQ
    c.1 ? v.1          -- input value from c.1 into v.1
    c.2 ! v.1          -- output value from v.1 to c.1
    c.3 ? b.1          -- input value from c.3 into b.1
    c.3 ? v.2          -- incorrect!
```

An example of use of channels is given below, where the two channels c.1 and c.2 which act as input and output channels respectively are defined as being channels of type integer. In general they may be specified by the following:

```
CHAN OF INT c.1,c.2:
```

where this definition may be in the outer body of the complete occam program. The use of these channels is then illustrated by the following process which sums up a sequence of numbers, and outputs their mean when it receives a negative number.

```
INT val, sum, count:
BOOL running:
SEQ
  running := TRUE
  count := 0
  sum := 0
  WHILE running
    SEQ
      c.1 ? val
      IF
        val > 0           -- accumulate the sum
          SEQ
            sum := sum + val
            count := count + 1
        val = 0           -- ignore this value
          SKIP
        val < 0           -- output the mean and terminate
          SEQ
            c.2 ! (sum/count)
            running := FALSE
```

The use of the type **BOOL** here is described in the next section. In this process the sum is accumulated from inputs on channel c.1 only for positive values of input. The values of zero are not included, although these could be regarded as contributing to the average value in which case a simple modification to the program can be made to achieve this. The mean value is output on channel c.2 when a negative value is input.

4.1.2 Boolean types

Values of the data type **BOOL** are either **TRUE** or **FALSE**. The values themselves are achieved as a result of some arithmetic operation and the results of this operation are then tested by one of a number of comparison operations. The following comparison tests, which can only be made between values of the same data types, are available within occam:

```
=       equal to
< >     not equal to
>       greater than
> =     greater than or equal to
<       less than
< =     less than or equal to
```

The values **TRUE** and **FALSE** are occam constants which themselves can be used in cases where a test is required. Examples of this are
given in the next section on replicators.

4.1.3 Constants

Constant values can have a name assigned to them by use of a specification
of the form

```
VAL type name IS value
```

For example, we could write:

```
VAL INT week IS 7 :
```

specifying that the data name is of type **INT** and has the constant value of 7.
In cases where the data type can be inferred from the data value itself then it
is allowed in occam for the data type itself not to be specified, so that a valid
alternative to the above would be:

```
VAL week IS 7 :
```

The process used to illustrate the use of channels can be modified to
illustrate an alternative of using constants. If the sending of a constant value,
−1 in this case, is used to indicate the end of the data stream input then the
process can be modified as follows.

```
INT val, sum, count:
BOOL running:
VAL INT terminate IS (-1):
SEQ
  running := TRUE
  count := 0
  sum := 0
  WHILE running
    SEQ
      c.1 ? val
      IF
        val = terminate    -- output the mean and terminate
```

```
          SEQ
            c.2 ! (sum/count)
            running := FALSE
      TRUE                        -- accumulate   the sum
        SEQ
          sum := sum + val
          count := count + 1
```

In the earlier version input values of zero were ignored; in this case the termination condition is put first in the body of the **IF**, and all other cases are handled in the alternative branch. A similar approach was one of the options that could have been used in the earlier example to overcome the input of values of zero.

4.1.4   Timer type

occam has a type **TIMER** allowing the creation of timers which can be used as clocks by processes. Timers are a primitive type, just like channels and data types, and the syntax is specified by

```
primitive.type =: TIMER
```

An operator **AFTER** can be used to compare times.

A timer is declared in a manner similar to channels and variables. For example in the case

```
TIMER clockA :
```

a timer is declared and identified by the name clockA. A value which is input from a timer provides a value of type **INT** representing time. The value is derived from a clock which changes by an increment at regular intervals. The rate at which the timer is incremented is dependent on the implementation. The value of the clock is cyclic; once it reaches a maximum positive integer value the next increment makes it the most negative value and the cycle is repeated.

Timers are accessed by using special input forms known as timer inputs, which are similar to channel inputs. The syntax for such timer inputs is given by

```
input         = timer input | delayed input
timer input   = timer ? variable
delayed input = timer ? AFTER expression
```

A timer input receives a value from the timer named on the left of the input symbol, ?, and assigns that value to the variable named on the right of the symbol. A delayed input waits until the value of the timer named to the left of the input symbol, ?, is later than the value of the expression on the right of the keyword **AFTER**.

In the following,

```
clockA ? time
```

inputs a value from the timer clockA and assigns it to the variable time. Inputs from the same timer may appear in any number of components in parallel, unlike inputs from channels.

In the following,

```
clockA ? AFTER time
```

the input waits until the value of the clockA is later than the value of time. An example of use to provide timer inputs at two defined points which are a fixed delay apart would be

```
SEQ
  clockA ? time
  clockA ? AFTER time PLUS  delay
```

Here a value representing the present time is input to the variable time. A further input after the value input from clockA is later than the value of time **PLUS** delay.

As an example of the use of a timer, this non-terminating process waits for a given time interval and the sends a 'time pulse' over a number of channels, represented by chan.1, ... ,chan.n.

```
VAL INT delay IS t:

TIMER clock.1:
INT time:
INT count:
SEQ
  count := 0
  clock.1 ? time
  WHILE TRUE
    SEQ
      time := time PLUS delay -- avoid arithmetic overflow
      clock.1 ? AFTER time    -- wait ...
      count := count + 1
      PAR                     -- send a number of messages
        chan.1 ! count        -- simultaneously
        ...
        chan.n ! count
```

There are two points to note about this program. Firstly, arithmetic on the time value is done using the **PLUS** operator instead of the usual '+' operator; the **PLUS** operator avoids arithmetic overflow, allowing the programmer to ignore the actual integer value of the time.

The second point to note is that the program avoids 'cumulative error'. If the program had taken the current value of the clock each time around the loop and then added the delay to it, then the clock pulses emerging from the process would have been separated by the delay plus the time required to send all of the messages. If the delay was small, this could introduce an appreciable error.

4.1.5 Characters

Occam does not have any type to represent alphabetic letters or words specifically. The representation of these will be discussed later, but for the present the comment can be made that characters are represented by numbers of type **BYTE**, and strings are represented as arrays of numbers of type **BYTE**.

4.2 Array types

In occam an array is a group of objects which are all of the same type. They are combined together into a single object with a name. Each of the objects in the array can be individually specified and referred to by specifying the appropriate subscript number to its position within the array. Each of these array elements is often referred to as a component of an array. The declaration of the array and its elements is similar in occam to other languages, though in this case the number of components in the array is contained in brackets which preceed the type. For example,

```
[50]INT total:   -- an array of fifty integers called total
```

The declaration of the array thus specifies both its size, or number of components, and its type.

In occam numbering starts with zero, so that the first component is component 0. Each component can be referred to, for example

```
total[6]              -- component 7
```

so that in the above array definition the components range from total[0] to total[49]. Attempts to use a subscript outside the range specified will cause an error; for example, total[50] would generate an error.

The components of array variables behave as ordinary variables and can be used in all places that variables can be used, in particular they can be assigned, input to, or output from, so that

```
chan3 ! total[4]    --output component 5 onto channel chan3
```

Whole arrays may also be assigned, input to, or output from, through channels provided the receiving variable is of the same type and the protocol of the channel being used is able to transmit that particular type.

Array types are constructed from *n* components of type T. An array type is a channel, timer or data type depending on the type of its components. Two arrays have the same type if they have the same number of components and the types of their components are the same. In the array type [e]T, the value of e defines the number of components in an array of the array type, and T defines the type of the components. Every array must have at least one component. A component of an array may be selected by subscription, so that

```
v[ e ]
```

selects the component e of v. A set of components of an array may also be selected by subscription. For example,

```
v[ FROM e FOR c ]
```

selects the components v[e], v[e + 1], ... v[e + c –1]. Here c specifies the number of components selected and not the maximum component value.

Variable arrays, record types and variant types can only be used in input and output. For variable arrays the representation is

```
array type = (type :: type).
```

For example, if I is an integer or byte type and A is an array type, then

```
(I :: A)
```

is the type of a record (*n*,*a*) in which *n* is a count of the number of components of *a*.

The following process is used as an illustration of the use of an array, in this case to store a sequence of values:

```
[80]INT values:
INT val, count:
BOOL running:
VAL INT dump.array IS -1:
VAL INT terminate IS -2:
SEQ
  running := TRUE
  count := 0
  WHILE running
    SEQ
      c1 ? val
```

```
    IF
      val = terminate
        running := FALSE
      val = dump.array
        INT ix:
        SEQ
          ix := 0
          WHILE ix < count
            SEQ
              c2 ! values[ix]
              ix := ix + 1
          count := 0
  TRUE
    SEQ
      values[count] := val
      count := count + 1
```

In this process values are accumulated in the array values, which are of type integer, so that the values which are used in the array, namely count and ix, both have to be of type integer. There is a limit of 80 for the size of the array set by the definition. Any attempt to read in data in excess of this will cause an error. In this illustration there are two termination conditions:

- the current contents of the array are output
- the execution is terminated

In the example the definition of the variable ix which is local to the output process is declared in the output process itself rather than in the body of the complete process.

occam allows the programmer to assign entire arrays, and sections of arrays, in a single assignment statement. For example, in order to assign the entire array a.2 to the array a.1, the programmer could write

```
[20]INT a.1, a.2:
SEQ
  a.1 := a.2
```

to assign the entire contents of a.2 to a.1; it is up to the occam translator to perform this as efficiently as possible.

It is also possible to use a slice of an array. For example, if we consider again the arrays a.1 and a.2 above, and we wish to copy the last five elements of array a.2 to the first five entries in a.1, then we can write

```
[20]INT a.1, a.2:
```

```
SEQ
    [a.1 FROM 0 FOR 5] := [a.2 FROM 15 FOR 5]
```

Again it is up to the occam translator to perform this as efficiently as possible. The bounds which are used in the array slice, namely 0 and 5 and 15 and 5, can be replaced by variables. The only restriction is that the lower bound, that is the starting point, must not be negative, and the upper bound, which is the length of the slice, must be greater than zero.

occam also allows the assignment of an array slice to a list of variables. For example, we can write

```
[20]INT a.1:
INT v.1, v.2, v.3:

SEQ
    [v.1, v.2, v.3] := [a.1 FROM 4 FOR  3]
```

which will result in the value of a.1[4] being assigned to the integer v.1, the value of a.1[5] being assigned to the integer v.2 and the value of a.1[6] being assigned to the integer v.3. Further discussion of this point will be made in Chapter 6.

4.3 Record types

Records are used to define structures whose components may be of different types. The syntax is given by

```
({,type})
```

For example,

```
RECORD Data.Collection IS   (INT,BYTE,BOOL) :
```

defines a record with three components, one of type **INT**, one of type **BYTE** and the third of type **BOOL**.

One of the major differences between occam and the more conventional languages, such as Pascal, is that record elements do not have names. Records are always manipulated in their entirety.

We can use and build a record in the following manner, where we have two records c.1 and c.2 with the same structure given Coord:

```
RECORD Coord IS (REAL32, REAL32, REAL32) :

Coord c.1, c.2:
REAL32 x, y, z:
```

```
SEQ
  c.1 := (1.0, 2.0, 3.0)
  (x, y, z) := c.1
  y    := y + 1.0 (REAL32)
  z    := z * 2.0 (REAL32)
  c.2 := (x, y, z)
```

occam also allows records to be nested, for example

```
RECORD Coord IS (REAL32, REAL32, REAL32) :
RECORD Item IS (BOOL, INT) :
RECORD Object IS (Item, Coord) :
```

Using the above illustration of records, it is possible to construct arrays of records, for example

```
[20] Coord List.Of.Coords:
```

would define an array List.Of.Coords where each element of the array is a record with three **REAL32**s.

5 occam processes

5.1 Language constructs

So far we have considered processes as being one of only three primitive kinds: assignment, input and output processes. A number of processes may be combined to form a construct. A construct is itself a process and so can be used to form part of a further construct. Each component process of a construct is written two spaces further from the left-hand margin, so as to indicate that it is part of the construct, and acts as a 'guard' for that particular construct.

In our notation a process can be written as

```
process = SKIP | STOP |   action | construction
```

```
         SKIP          starts a process, performs no action
                       and terminates
         STOP          starts a process but never proceeds
                       and never terminates.
```

SKIP can be considered as a process that does nothing, so that it can be used to stand in for parts of a program which may not be written but which for the time being can be allowed to do nothing. Equally it is often used to satisfy conditions in some of the constructs to be described.

STOP can be considered as representing a process which does not work, and as such could be used in program development to replace a process which has yet to be written. It is important to realise that a stopped process cannot proceed and in particular never terminates. For example, a process may become stopped waiting for input which will never come and hence the process becomes deadlocked. Correct termination of concurrent processes is most important.

The difference between the **SKIP** and **STOP** processes can be illustrated in the following sequence:

```
SEQ
  keyboard ? char
```

```
SKIP
screen ! char
```

```
SEQ
  keyboard ? char
  STOP
  screen ! char
```

In the first case the sequence is such that a variable called char is input via the channel keyboard. When this process terminates the process **SKIP**, which performs no action, is then executed. This is followed by outputting the variable char through the channel screen.

In the second case the sequence again starts by inputting the variable called char via the channel keyboard. When this process terminates the process **STOP** then executes which does not terminate so that the sequence cannot continue and the statement

```
screen ! char
```

is never executed.

Several processes may be combined into a larger process by the same specification as to how the processes are to be performed. For example, the specification could be that the processes may need to be performed one after the other, i.e. in sequence, or all at the same time, i.e. in parallel. Construction may be represented in the form:

```
construction = sequence | parallel | conditional | loop |
               alternation
```

The classes of constructs are then given by:

- **SEQ** sequence
- **PAR** parallel
- **IF** conditional
- **WHILE** loop
- **ALT** alternation

and these are now considered in more detail.

5.1.1 SEQ sequence

The sequential construct can be represented by

```
sequence = SEQ
               {process}
```

The **SEQ** construct is followed by one or more processes which are indented by two spaces. For example,

```
SEQ
  P1
  P2
  P3
  . . .
```

means that the processes P1, P2, P3, ... are executed one after the other. Each process starts only when the one above it has terminated, so that in this case the order is process P1 followed by process P2, and so on. The whole sequence terminates when the last process has itself terminated. A sequence with no component processes behaves like **SKIP**. For example,

```
SEQ
  c.1 ? x
  x := x + 1
  c.2 ! x
```

inputs a value on channel c.1 to the variable x. Then x is incremented by 1, and finally the result is output on channel c.2.

5.1.2 PAR parallel

A parallel construct can be represented by

```
parallel = PAR
              {process}
```

The **PAR** construct is followed by zero or more processes which are indented by two spaces. For example,

```
PAR
  P1
  P2
  P3
  . . .
```

means that the processes P1, P2, P3, ... start simultaneously, and proceed together, and therefore the processes must be independent of each other. The construct terminates only after all the component processes have terminated, but there is no fixed order in which the individual processes will terminate. A parallel process is ready to communicate on a channel if any of its components is ready. A parallel construct with no component processes behaves like **SKIP**.

There are several important constraints on the parallel construct relating to the independence of its constituent processes. No variable changed by assignment or input in any component processes of a parallel construct may be used in any other component of the same construct. Within the same construct no channel may be used for input in more than one component process and no channel may be used for output in more than one component process. A parallel construct is invalid unless these non-interference conditions are satisfied. The sequence

```
PAR
   c.1 ? x
   c.2 ! y
```

allows the communications of input on channel c.1 of the variable x, and the output on the channel c.2 of the variable y, to take place together i.e. concurrently. This parallelism is highly optimised in order to incur minimal process scheduling.

5.1.3 PLACED PAR

Once a program has been developed and verified then the component processes may each be executed on a individual processor. A variant of the **PAR** construct called the **PLACED PAR** is used to assign a process for execution to a specified processor. The syntax for this construct is

```
parallel = PLACED PAR
                {placement}
            | PLACED PAR replicator
              placement
placement = PROCESSOR expression
              process
```

For example,

```
PLACED PAR
   PROCESSOR 1
      P1
   PROCESSOR 2
      P2
```

means that the processes P1 and P2 are placed on the individual processors numbered 1 and 2 respectively.

5.1.4 IF conditional

A conditional construct can be represented as

```
conditional = IF
                  {choice}
```

```
choice = guarded.choice | conditional

guarded.choice =: boolean
                   process
boolean = expression
```

A choice is either a guarded choice or a further conditional. A guarded choice is itself a boolean followed by a process which is indented by two spaces. For example,

```
condition1
  P1
condition2
  P2

...
```

is such that, if P1 and P2 are processes and condition1 and condition2 represent conditions whose values may be either **TRUE** or **FALSE**, then P1 is executed if condition1 is **TRUE**, otherwise P2 is executed if condition2 is **TRUE**, and so on for any other conditions. Only one of the processes is executed and then the construct terminates. Notice the indentation of P1 and P2 as described before. A conditional behaves like the first of the choices that can proceed, or like **STOP** if none of them can proceed. For example,

```
IF
  x = 0
    y := y + 1
  x <> 0
    SKIP
```

increments the value of the variable y if and only if $x = 0$. There is a need to provide an option if $x <> 0$ and this is achieved by use of the **SKIP** command.

A conditional construct with no component choices behaves like **STOP**. If in the above example the coding is altered to

```
IF
  x = 0
    y := y + 1
```

then in this case, where the **IF** statement only has one component, then for the case $x <> 0$ the conditional behaves as the primitive **STOP**. It is often convenient to use a 'catch all' situation, so that in the following the boolean constant **TRUE** is always true and used to provide an 'otherwise' condition where neither $x < 0$ nor $x > 0$ is satisfied.

```
IF
  x < 0
    z := y - 1
  x > 0
    z := y + 1
  TRUE
    z := y
```

5.1.5 WHILE loop

The loop construct can be represented by

```
loop    = WHILE boolean
              process
```

The **WHILE** command is followed, to its right, by a boolean expression, and this is followed on the next line by a process which is indented by two spaces. For example,

```
WHILE
  P1
```

means that the process P1 is continuously executed while the value of the condition is **TRUE** and only terminates when the condition becomes **FALSE**. This means that

```
WHILE (x - 5) > 0
  x := x - 5
```

leaves x with the value of (x MOD 5) if x is positive.

The following process, which was considered in Chapter 4 for the case of arrays, also serves to illustrate the use of the WHILE construct.

```
[80]INT values:
INT val, count:
BOOL running:
VAL INT dump.array IS -1:
VAL INT terminate IS -2:
SEQ
  running := TRUE
  count := 0
  WHILE running
    SEQ
      cl ? val
      IF
        val = terminate
```

```
        running := FALSE
    val = dump.array
      INT ix:
      SEQ
        ix := 0
        WHILE ix < count
          SEQ
            c2 ! values[ix]
            ix := ix + 1
        count := 0
  TRUE
    SEQ
      values[count] := val
      count := count + 1
```

5.1.6 ALT alternation

An alternative construct may be represented by

```
alternation         =  ALT
                          {alternative}

alternative         =  guarded.alternative | alternation

guarded.alternative =  guard
                         process

guard               =  input|boolean & input|boolean & SKIP
```

The **ALT** construct is followed by one or more alternative processes which are indented by two spaces. An alternative may be either a guarded alternative or another alternation. A guarded alternative is an input, or a boolean expression to the left of the ampersand, &, with an input or **SKIP** on the right. **SKIP** can take the place of an input in a guard which includes a boolean expression. For example,

```
ALT
  input1
    P1
  input2
    P2
  input3
    P3
  ...
```

where P1, P2 and P3 are processes and input1, input2, input3, ... usually refer to input processes, but can be output processes, is such that the process waits until one of the input processes input1, input2, input3, ..., is ready. If input1 becomes ready first then process P1 will be executed. Similarly if input2 becomes ready first, then process P2 will be executed, and so on. Only one of the processes will be executed and the process terminates when that process which has been chosen is itself terminated. A guard behaves as **STOP** if its boolean is initially **FALSE**, and like the input or **SKIP** otherwise. An alternation with no component alternatives behaves as a **STOP**. For example,

```
ALT
  count ? signal
    counter := counter + 1
  total ? signal
    SEQ
      out ! counter
      counter := 0
```

executes one or other of the following:

- inputs a signal from channel count, then increments the value of the variable counter
- inputs a signal on the channel total, then outputs on the channel out the value of the variable counter, and finally resets the value of the counter to zero.

Guards in **ALT** statements have a number of uses, one of which might be to ignore certain channels. For instance,

```
CHAN OF INT c.1, c.2, c.3:
INT input:
BOOL running, flag:

SEQ
  running, flag := TRUE, TRUE
  WHILE running
    SEQ
      ALT
        flag & c.1 ? input
          c.3 ! input
        flag & c.2 ? input
          c.3 ! input
        NOT flag & c.1 ? input
```

```
c.3 ! input
```

```
-- code that alters running and flag
```

This process will look for input on two channels, c.1 and c.2. While flag is **TRUE**, both c.1 and c.2 will be read and passed on unchanged. However, when flag is **FALSE**, c.2 will be ignored and only c.1 will be passed on.

It is important to remember that one of the guards must be true – if all the guards are false, the **ALT** statement becomes equivalent to **STOP**, which in most cases is probably not what was intended.

5.1.7 CASE

The constructs of **IF**, **WHILE** and **ALT** provide a means of selection between processes dependent on conditional selection criteria. Another construct exists which provides a further selection option, and that is the **CASE** construct. This can be represented as

```
selection   = CASE selector
                {option}
```

```
option      = {1,case.expression}
                process
            | ELSE
                process
```

```
selector       = expression
case.expression = expression
```

The keyword **CASE** is followed by one or more options which are indented by two spaces. Each option starts with either a list of case expressions or the keyword **ELSE**. However, each selection may only have one **ELSE** option. The option is followed by a process which is itself indented by a further two spaces. All case expressions used in a selection must have distinct constant values, so that there is no ambiguity between values used in the selection. The selector and case expressions must be of the same data type, which may be either **INT** or **BYTE**.

In this case the selector is evaluated, and its value is used to select one of the component selections. If the value of the selector is the same as one of the values of the expressions then that expression is selected and the **CASE** behaves as the process in that selection. Otherwise the selection behaves as the process in the **ELSE** selection. If there is no **ELSE** selection and the **CASE** does not select any of the other processes then the construct behaves as a **STOP**.

In the following example,

```
CASE number
  '1', '3', '5', '7', '9'
    odd := TRUE
```

the **CASE** construct is such that that if number has the character values of 1, 3, 5, 7, 9 then the variable odd is returned as **TRUE**, otherwise the selection behaves as the primitive process **STOP**. As discussed elsewhere, it is often desirable to have an option which allows all possible selections to be covered. The above program could be modified:

```
CASE number
  '1', '3', '5', '7', '9'
    odd := TRUE
  ELSE
    odd := FALSE
```

where the **ELSE** will only be effective when no other selection is satisfied.

5.2 Replicators

So far we have discussed the constructs **SEQ, PAR, IF, WHILE** and **ALT**. In order to repeat a process a number of times, a construct exists which can be used to provide replication of a process.

In general, if X represents one of constructs **SEQ, PAR, IF,** or **ALT** and Z(n) is a corresponding process and A and B are expressions of type **INT** with values a and b then the form of the replicator construct can be given by

```
X n = A FOR B
  Z (n)
```

The meaning of the replicator can now be expressed as:

```
SEQ n = A FOR 0      =>     SKIP
  Z (n)

PAR n = A FOR 0      =>     SKIP
  Z (n)

IF  n = A FOR 0      =>     STOP
  Z (n)

ALT n = A FOR 0      =>     STOP
  Z (n)
```

If B > 0 then

```
X n = A FOR B        => X
                         Z(a)
                         Z(a + 1)
                         ...
                         Z(a + b - 1)
```

If B < 0 then

```
X n = A FOR B        is invalid
  Z(n)
```


5.2.1 Replicated SEQ

The syntax of the replicated **SEQ** extends the syntax of the **SEQ** construct
which was discussed in an earlier section. The syntax is represented by

```
sequence = SEQ replicator
              process
replicator = name = base FOR count
base        = expression
count       = expression
```

In this construct the **SEQ** and the replicator, which is written to the right
of the **SEQ**, are followed by a process which is indented by two spaces. The
replicator specifies the name for the index, which does not need to be
declared elsewhere. The value of the index for the first replication is the
value of the base expression, and the number of times that the process is
replicated is the value of the count expression at the start of the sequence.
The index, which has a value of type **INT**, can be used in the expression but
it cannot be assigned to by an input or an assignment. The base and count
expressions are also of type **INT**. A value for count such that count < 0 is
invalid, and the case where count = 0 means that the replicated **SEQ**
sequence behaves like the primitive process **SKIP**.

The replicated **SEQ** construct is equivalent to a counted loop. For
example,

```
SEQ i = 0 FOR n
  P1
```

causes the process P1 to be repeated n times. If input is specified as a
channel, then

```
INT y:
SEQ i = 0 FOR 10
  input ? y
```

means 'produce ten replicas of the input process and execute them in sequence'. An alternative piece of code to achieve the same result without use of the replication construct might be

```
INT y,i:
SEQ
  i := 0
  WHILE i < 10
    SEQ
      input ? y
      i := i + 1
```

It is clear that use of the replicator is more concise and does not need the declaration of a separate loop counter variable, i in this case, and its subsequent incrementing each time the loop is executed.

Since the use of replicated **SEQ** constitutes an array of processes, the construct can only terminate once all the processes in the array have finished. This means that partial execution of the replicated **SEQ** is invalid, as is partial execution of any of the other replicated constructs.

We can use the replicated **SEQ** to rewrite the example used in section 4.2:

```
[80]INT values:
INT val, count:
BOOL running:

VAL INT dump.array IS -1:
VAL INT terminate IS -2:

SEQ
  running := TRUE
  count := 0
  WHILE running
    SEQ
      c.1 ? val
      IF
        val = terminate
          running := FALSE
        val = dump.array
          SEQ
            SEQ ix = 0 FOR  count - 1
              c.2 ! values[ix]
              ix := ix + 1
            count := 0
        TRUE
          SEQ
```

```
values[count] := val
count := count + 1
```

As before, the channels c.1 and c.2 are declared elsewhere in the program. The explicit loop that was used previously has now been replaced by the replicated **SEQ**. Not only does this shorten the program, but it also makes the meaning slightly more clear.

5.2.2 Replicated PAR

The syntax for the replicated **PAR** is similar to that just described for the replicated **SEQ**:

```
parallel    = PAR replicator
                  process
replicator  = name = base FOR count
base        = expression
count       = expression
```

The **PAR** and the replicator, which is written to the right of the **PAR**, is followed by a process which is indented by two spaces. The replicator specifies the name for the index, which does not need to be declared elsewhere. The value of the index for the first replication is the value of the base expression, and the number of times that the process is replicated is the value of the count expression at the start of the sequence. The index, which has a value of type **INT**, can be used in the expression but it cannot be assigned to by an input or an assignment. The base and count expressions are also of type **INT**, and must be constant values. A value for count such that count < 0 is invalid, and the case where count $= 0$ means that the replicated **PAR** sequence behaves like the primitive process **SKIP**.

The replicated **PAR** construct produces an array of structurally similar parallel processes. It is used in a wide range of applications, and it provides an easy implementation of such concepts as queues, buffers and pipelines. In general for the replicated **PAR** construct we could have,

```
PAR i = 0 FOR n
  Pi
```

which constructs an array of n similar processes $P_0, P_1, .. P_{n-1}$.

As an illustration of the construct, we consider implementation of a simple queue. Queues are often used as a way of buffering between processes, when they operate in such a way that the rate of supply and demand between processes is not equal, and data needs to be temporarily stored before processing. This effect can be easily simulated as data passing down a chain of buckets, or slots in the program. The slots form an array of parallel processors which pass data between the slots. A typical program might be

```
[20] CHAN OF INT slot:
PAR i := 0 FOR 19
  WHILE TRUE
    INT y :
    SEQ
      slot[i] ? y
      slot[i + 1] ! y
```

Here 19 parallel processes are set up which continually transfer data between slots in the queue. The queue is represented by an array of 20 channels. Note that the synchronisation between successive slots is achieved within the SEQ construct. However, this can only be regarded as a part of a program since by itself it does not provide a satisfactory initial source of data into slot[0] or indeed an effective output for data from slot[20]. This provision would need to be provided elsewhere within a complete program, since this fragment of code simply illustrates the use of the parallel construct for an array of processes.

This example could make use of channel constants as follows:

```
[20] CHAN OF INT slot:

PAR i := 0 FOR (SIZE slot - 1)
  VAL input IS slot[i]:
  VAL output IS slot[i + 1]:
  WHILE TRUE
    INT y:
    SEQ
      input ? y
      output ! y
```

Here we define two channel constants, input and output, to correspond to two elements in the slot array. This technique of defining a constant to be an array element has two advantages. Firstly, it can make large code segments more readable by giving names to global items; this is particularly true for pipelines of processes, where the processes are working on sections of a large volume of data. Secondly, the occam translator can calculate the offset into the array, which in this case is slot, only once; as a result, the constant names are more efficient.

In order to illustrate the use of the replicated PAR we consider a case where we want to build a pipeline of filter processes which will look for data values, as illustrated in figure 5.1. Each stage of the pipeline must do one of three things:

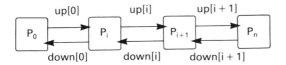

Each process i reads from up[i − 1] and writes to up[i].
Each process i reads from down[i] and writes to down[i − 1].

Figure 5.1 Illustration of a pipeline

- count an item
- pass an item on
- pass the item count to a receiving process and terminate

We assume a number of global declarations as follows,

```
VAL scan.values IS [ ... ]:
```

```
CHAN OF INT in[SIZE scan.values+1]:
CHAN OF INT collect[SIZE scan.values]:
```

Here scan.values is an array of data items to look for, in is an array of channels for passing data in and out of pipeline stages and collect is an array of channels for collecting the item counts.

The pipeline can then look like this:

```
VAL INT terminate IS -1:

PAR ix = 0 FOR (SIZE scan.values-1)
  INT item:
  INT count:
  BOOL running:

  VAL input IS in[ix]:
  VAL output IS in[ix+1]:
  VAL myvalue IS scan.values[ix]:

SEQ
  running := TRUE
  count := 0
  WHILE running
    SEQ
      input ? item
```

```
IF·
  item = terminate
    SEQ
      output ! terminate
      collect[ix] ! count
      running := FALSE
  item = myvalue
    count := count + 1
  TRUE
    output ! item
```

Whilst this represents code for the pipeline process, the pipeline itself will be embedded in a larger program which includes a data source, a data sink, and a count collector. The data item that closes down the pipeline, namely terminate, must be passed onto the next stage. The data source passes a terminate item into the pipeline and the pipeline closes down in sequence. In a later section the collection of program fragments together to form procedures will be discussed, and a more elegant solution to this problem will be presented.

It should be remembered that, as discussed in the last chapter, components of arrays in occam begin at zero. This affects use of arrays in replicated statements. An array like scan.values which is declared as

```
CHAN OF INT in[SIZE x]:
```

is indexed from in[0] up to [SIZE x–1]. This means that care must be taken in the VAL declarations, since this aspect of array declarations affects the program quite considerably.

5.2.3 Replicated IF

The syntax for the replicated IF is the following:

```
conditional = IF' replicator
                choice
replicator  = name = base FOR count
base        = expression
count       = expression
```

The keyword IF and the replicator, which is to the right of the keyword, are followed by a choice which is indented by two spaces. The replicator specifies the name for the index which does not need to be declared elsewhere. The value of the index for the first replication is the value of the base expression, and the number of times that the process is replicated is the value of the count expression at the start of the sequence. The index, which has a value of type INT, can be used in the expression but it cannot be assigned to by an input or an assignment. The base and count expressions are also of type **INT**, and must be constant values. A value for count such that count < 0 is invalid, and the case count = 0 means that the replicated **IF** sequence behaves like the primitive process **STOP**.

The replicated **IF** produces a conditional construct with a number of choices which are similarly structured. For example,

```
IF i = 0 FOR 3
  array[i] = 0
    array[i] := 1
```

would check the first three elements of the array for a zero. The first element which it finds to be zero it will replace with a one. One of the problems of this program fragment is that if no element is found to contain a zero the program will stop. We would like to conclude the replication with a **TRUE SKIP**, but as stated earlier no replication construct can be only partially executed. A solution to the problem is to us the concept of 'nesting' the replicated **IF** construct within another **IF** construct, for example:

```
IF
  IF i = 0 FOR 3
    array[i] = 0
      array[i + 1] := 1
  TRUE
    SKIP
```

which will now execute the **SKIP** if no zeroes are found. The program will continue after the replication whether or not a zero is found in the elements of the array.

An examination of the formal definition of the replicated **IF** statement will reveal that it evaluates its conditions in sequence, looking for the first one that is true. This suggests an elegant solution to a common programming problem, namely that of finding the first element of an array that obeys some rule. For instance, suppose that we want to find the first non-zero element in an integer array, called items:

```
[ ]INT items: -- array of integers
INT first.non.zero:

IF
  IF i = 0 FOR SIZE items
    items[i] <> 0
      first.non.zero := i
  TRUE
    first.non.zero := -1
```

Here, we simply create a replicated **IF** over the elements of the array. If there is a non-zero item, its index will be returned in first.non.zero. If the array is all-zero, then the **TRUE** branch will return an index of –1. Note that if the **TRUE** branch was missing and the array was all-zero then the replicated **IF** would be equivalent to **STOP**.

5.2.4 Replicated ALT

The syntax for the replicated **ALT** is

```
alternation = ALT replicator
                  alternative
replicator  = name = base FOR count
base        = expression
count       = expression
```

The keyword **ALT** and the replicator, which is to the right of the keyword, are followed by the alternative which is indented by two spaces. The replicator specifies the name for the index, which does not need to be declared elsewhere. The value of the index for the first replication is the value of the base expression, and the number of times that the process is replicated is the value of the count expression at the start of the sequence. The index, which has a value of type **INT**, can be used in the expression but it cannot be assigned to by an input or an assignment. The base and count expressions are also of type **INT**, and must be constant values. A value for count such that count < 0 is invalid, and the case count = 0 means that the replicated **ALT** sequence behaves like the primitive process **STOP**.

A replicated **ALT** consists of a number of identically structured alternative constructs, each of which is triggered by input from a channel. For example, a program fragment that would act as a multiplexer might be

```
[40]CHAN OF INT in :
CHAN OF INT out :
PAR
   ...processes providing data on in channels
   WHILE TRUE
     INT y :
     ALT i = 0 FOR 40
       in[i] ? y
         out ! y
   ...processes taking data from out channel
```

This monitors 40 input channels; when any one of them has any data the data is passed to the out channel. Hence communication from the 40 channels is merged into the out channel. This illustration of multiplexing of data forms the basis of many applications in the control and switching of networks, and the monitoring of equipment.

5.3 Priorities

5.3.1 PRI PAR

The **PAR** construct is such that a number of concurrently executing processes can be generated. The amount of time that each of the processes gets is dependent on the scheduling algorithm that is used in the runtime system. This means that the **PAR** construct is implementation-dependent. It is often useful to be able to specify that out of a series of processes which can run concurrently there is a measure of priority about their allocation. In this way a high-priority process will have preference over a low-priority process provided they are executing on the same processor. The syntax for the priority execution of parallel processes is

```
parallel  = PRI PAR
              {process}
          | PRI PAR replicator
              process
```

where the keywords **PRI PAR** are followed by zero or more processes which are indented by two spaces. The process may be replicated as described in section 5.2. For example,

```
PRI PAR
  P1          -- process with highest priority
  PAR         -- two processes of equal priority
    P2
    P3
  P4          -- process of lowest priority
```

The ordering of priority is taken from the order in which the processes are written, so that in the above example the process P1 has the highest priority and the process P4 the lowest. If processes are to have equal priority then they can be constructed into a parallel construct within the **PRI PAR,** so that in the above example the two processes P2 and P3 have equal priority, at an intermediate level between the high priority of P1 and the low priority of P4.

The **PRI PAR** is very useful in real-time applications where we can allocate the highest priority to the process that has to handle a response, and the programmer can then ensure that the other processes are not executed until the real-time event has been handled. On a transputer only two priority levels are supported, and in general the fact that the runtime system has to support distinct queues for each priority means that this construct is implementation-dependent.

The **PRI PAR** statement can be used to allow rapid response to urgent events happening elsewhere. For instance, we could write,

```
[3]CHAN OF INT priority:

PRI PAR i = 0 FOR SIZE priority
  INT value:
  SEQ
    priority[i] ? value

    -- code to handle message of priority i
```

In this case notice that each handler process will be based on the same occam code, but will run independently. If we wanted each priority level to be handled in a different manner we would have to write

```
PRI PAR
  INT value:
  SEQ
    priority[0] ? value

    -- code for priority 0
  INT value:
  SEQ
    priority[1] ? value

    -- code for priority 1
  INT value:
  SEQ
    priority[2] ? value

    -- code for priority 2
```

where 0 is the highest priority level and 2 is the lowest level.

As another example, we might wish to respond to timeouts very rapidly while handling other messages in a more leisurely manner; consider the following:

```
CHAN OF INT request:
PRI PAR
  TIMER clock:
  VAL INT delay IS t:
  INT time:
  SEQ                       -- wait for timeouts
    clock ? time
    WHILE TRUE
      SEQ
        time := time PLUS delay
```

```
clock ? AFTER time
```

```
- respond to timeout
```

```
INT value:
SEQ - wait for lower priority requests
request ? value
```

```
- respond to request
```

5.3.2 PRI ALT

In section 5.1 we considered the construct to provide the option of selection of alternative processes, namely the **ALT** construct. Just as with the **PRI PAR** where we are able to give a priority to processes which are to be executed in parallel, so with the **PRI ALT** we have the ability to give priority in execution to a series of alternatives. The syntax for the construct is given by

```
alternation  = PRI ALT
                   {alternative}
             | PRI ALT replicator
                   alternative
```

where the keywords **PRI ALT** are followed by zero or more processes which are indented by two spaces. As with the **ALT** construct described earlier in section 5.1, the alternative may be replicated. For example:

```
PRI ALT
  stream ? blocks
    SKIP
  TRUE & SKIP
    P1
```

In this case the process inputs blocks if an input from channel stream is ready, otherwise if the boolean **TRUE** is valid then the process P1 is executed. The use of the **TRUE & SKIP** guard in the **PRI ALT** construct has many uses.

In some senses the **PRI PAR** appears as an alternative to the **PRI ALT** statement. However, they have very different semantics. The **PRI PAR** statement produces a number of independent processes running at various priority levels; the **PRI ALT** statement produces a single process which waits for input events at various priority levels. For example, consider the following:

```
[3]CHAN OF INT priority:

PRI ALT i = 0 FOR SIZE  priority
  INT value:
  SEQ
    priority[i] ? value

    -- message handling code
```

Comparing this with the example in the previous section shows that here we have one process which is waiting on a number of channels, whereas in the previous section we had a number of processes waiting on a number of channels simultaneously.

5.4 Protocol

We have already described how a channel is used to communicate between two concurrent processes. The format and data type of these channels is specified by the channel protocol. This protocol is specified when the channel is declared. The definition has to be such that the input and output using the channel must be compatible with the channel protocol specified for that channel. Thus channel protocols allow the compiler to check on the correct use of the channels. The simplest protocols have already been described and consist of a primitive data type, such as a byte protocol, or an array data type. The syntax for simple protocols is

```
simple.protocol = type
                | primitive.type :: []type
input           = channel ? input.item
input.item      = variable
                | variable :: variable
output          = channel ! output.item
output.item     = variable
                | expression :: expression
protocol        = simple.protocol
```

So a simple protocol is either a data type or a counted array as specified by the data type of the count, which can be either an integer or byte, followed by a double colon, square brackets and a specifier indicating the type of the components. For example, for the declaration of

```
CHAN OF INT::[]BYTE mail :
```

declares a channel called mail which outputs first an integer, then that number of items from an array as specified by this integer. If an output on this channel is given by

```
mail ! 11::"The machine needs updating"
```

the effect of the declaration will be to output the first 11 characters of the message, namely 'The machine'.

It is often convenient to give a name to a protocol, and this can be done in a protocol definition. The syntax for this is

```
definition = PROTOCOL name IS simple.protocol
           | PROTOCOL name IS sequential.protocol
protocol   = name
```

A protocol defines the name, which appears to the right of the keyword **IS** if a simple protocol as described above is used or that of a sequential protocol which will be described in the next section. Whilst the definition occurs on a single line and is terminated by a colon, the line may be broken after the keyword **IS** or after a semicolon in a sequential protocol. For example, in the definition

```
PROTOCOL CHAR IS BYTE :
```

a channel with the protocol **CHAR** can then be declared as

```
CHAN OF CHAR mail :
```

5.4.1 Sequential protocol

Having established simple protocols, a sequence of such protocols can be defined by means of the sequential protocol definition. The syntax for this is

```
sequential.protocol = {1;simple protocol}
input               = channel ? {1;input.item}
input.item          = variable
                    | variable :: variable
output              = channel ! {1;output.item}
output.item         = variable
                    | expression :: expression
```

A sequential protocol is one or more simple protocols separated by semi-colons, and the definition is terminated with a colon. The communications on a channel are then valid provided that the type of the input and output on that channel are compatible with the corresponding component of the protocol. For example,

```
PROTOCOL COORDINATE IS REAL32; REAL32; REAL32 :
```

allows channels to be declared with this protocol which will pass values in groups of threes. The definition

```
CHAN OF COORDINATE data :
```

would, for example, allow input on the channel data in a form

```
data ? xvalue; yvalue; zvalue
```

where each value is input in sequence and assigned to each variable in turn.

5.4.2 Variant types

Although we have so far emphasised the need for the data transmitted via a channel to be of the same type as the definition of the channel via which the communication is to take place, it is often useful to be able to communicate through a single channel data which is of different formats. To provide this facility, variant protocol allows the definition of a channel protocol to specify a number of possible formats that may be used with a given communication channel. The definition of the variant protocol is different for the situations of input and output. We consider first the case of output, for which the syntax for the variant protocol is

```
definition        = PROTOCOL name
                      CASE
                        {tagged.protocol}
                    :
tagged.protocol = tag
                  | tag;sequential.protocol
tag               = name
output            = channel ! tag
                  | channel ! tag;{1;output.item}
output.item       = variable
                  | expression :: expression
```

Here the name defined by the variant protocol appears to the right of the keyword **PROTOCOL**, which is followed by the keyword **CASE** at an indentation of two spaces. The keyword **CASE** is then followed at an indentation of a further two spaces by a series of tagged protocols. The definition is finally terminated by a colon, which is on a line by itself at the same level of indentation as the character **P** of **PROTOCOL**. A tagged protocol is either a tag by itself or a tag followed by a semicolon and a sequential protocol. Tags themselves are names which must be distinct and must be defined only within the variant protocol. In the case of output on a channel of variant protocol the output is a tag by itself, or it is a tag followed by a series of output items which are each separated from each other by semicolons. The output is then valid only if the tag or the associated output items are compatible with one of the tagged protocols specified in the definition.

As an example, consider the possible requirement to output data which may be either of type **INT** or type **REAL32**:

```
PROTOCOL INT.OR.REAL
  CASE
    Fixed ; INT
    Floating ; REAL32
  :
CHAN OF INT.OR.REAL chanvalue :
PAR
  SEQ
    chanvalue ! Fixed; I      -- integer
    chanvalue ! Floating; R   -- real
```

Here the channel chanvalue is used to communicate a value of type **INT** or type **REAL32**.

So far we have considered the use of variant protocol for output. For input the situation is rather more complicated. This is because the reading process does not know the type of object which is being transmitted and therefore it has to have a series of possible read actions depending on the type of the data, one for each tag field. The syntax for the variant protocol in this case is

```
case.input       = channel ? CASE
                     {variant}
variant          = tagged.list
                     process
                 | specification
                   variant
tagged.list      = tag
                 | tag;{1;input.item}
input.item       = variable
                 | variable :: variable
process          = case.input
input            = channel ? CASE tagged.list
```

A case input receives a tag from the channel which is named to the left of the case input symbol '? **CASE**', and this tag is then used to select from one of the variants. These variants appear on the following lines indented by two spaces. When a tag is input, if the variant with that tag is present then the process next inputs the remainder of the tagged list, and an associated process which is indented by a further two spaces is performed. If no variant with that tag is found the process next behaves like the primitive process **STOP**. A case input may only consist of a tagged list.

For example, if we wish to modify the earlier code to allow the input of values which may be tagged to be of type **INT** or **REAL32**, we could have

```
PROTOCOL INT.OR.REAL
  CASE
    Fixed ; INT
    Floating ; REAL32
  :
CHAN OF INT.OR.REAL chanvalue :
PAR
  SEQ                              -- process for output
    chanvalue ! Fixed; I      -- integer
    chanvalue ! Floating; R  -- real
  SEQ                              -- process for input
    chanvalue ? CASE
      Fixed ; J
        This.Is.An.Integer := TRUE
      Floating ; S
        This.Is.An.Integer := FALSE
```

This will either read a value of type **INT** into J via channel chanvalue, and set the boolean This.Is.An.Integer to **TRUE**, or read a value of type **REAL32** into R via the same channel chanvalue and set the boolean This.Is.An.-Integer to **FALSE**. Only one of these actions will take place before the case input process terminates. If neither of the appropriate tag values is found then the case input process behaves as the primitive process **STOP**.

Whilst the use of variant protocol allows the selection between several different data types for input and output via a communication channel, there can be occasions where we seek to specify a channel protocol where the format for that channel cannot be defined. An example of this situation could be communicating with external devices such as printers and terminals. This means that the compiler does not perform runtime checks or detect any errors if the channel is misused. The channel protocol definition is given by

```
CHAN OF ANY :
```

For example,

```
CHAN OF ANY terminal:
PLACE terminal AT 1:
```

is the definition that has to be used to map data onto a terminal screen. This is a historical reason, and the use of the definition **CHAN OF ANY** is not recommended for common use.

In an ISO-type protocol handler, which is illustrated in figure 5.2, the physical communication channel can be viewed as a nested series of channels, each with its own protocols. In the diagram, data flowing from level 2, for example, will be wrapped up in the protocol of layer 1; the resulting data will be wrapped up in the protocol of layer 0 and then transmitted over the physical channel. The receiving end unwraps the protocol, layer by layer, with each layer collecting the appropriate data. This allows the various layers to communicate without concern for the layers below them, other than assuming that such layers exist.

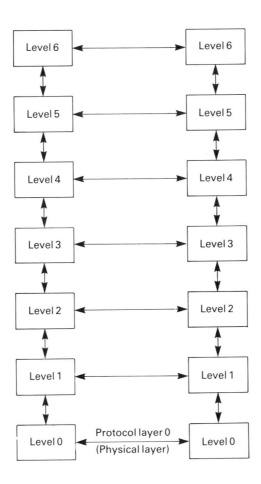

Figure 5.2 Illustration of an ISO-type protocol handler

Variant protocols allow the programmer to explicitly define messages which are 'out of band' — that is, they are control messages rather than data messages. In this case each handler may want to send messages to the corresponding message handler on the far end of the communication channel. One approach would be to encode the messages in some other way using the existing channel protocol. For example, on a **CHAN OF INT**, we could encode a control message by prefixing it with four −1 values followed by an integer representing the message; however, if the user of the channel ever decides to send four −1 values as data then trouble is likely to ensue.

An alternative, and safer, approach is to use a variant protocol. For example,

```
PROTOCOL Int.Or.Message
  CASE
    Flush.Buffer
    Close.Channel
    Message; INT
    Value; INT
  :
```

```
CHAN OF INT Int.Or.Message chan:
```

We can handle such a protocol at the receiving end as follows:

```
INT message.value:
INT  val:
SEQ
  chan ? CASE
    Flush.Buffer
      -- code to flush the input buffer
    Close.Channel
      -- terminate this listening process
    Message: message.value
      -- act on the message
    Value; val
      -- pass the value on
```

Using a variant protocol, we can rewrite the example in section 5.1.5 as follows:

```
PROTOCOL Int.Or.Message
  CASE
    Dump.Array
    Terminate
    Int.Value; INT
  :
```

```
CHAN OF Int.Or.Message chan:
CHAN OF INT output:
[n]INT values:
INT value, count:
BOOL running:

SEQ
  running := TRUE
  count := 0
  WHILE running
    SEQ
      chan ? CASE
        Int.Value; value
          SEQ
            values[count] := value
            count := count + 1
        Terminate
          running := FALSE
        Dump.Array
          SEQ
            SEQ ix = 0 FOR count
              output ! values[ix]
            count := 0
```

It is left to the reader to decide which version, the one given here or those presented in sections 5.1.5 and 5.2.1, is the most readable and reliable.

6 Expressions

In the previous chapter we used the term 'expression' without detailed discussion of the range of operations that can be covered in occam. In its simplest form an expression has been regarded as performing an evaluation and producing a result. The result of an expression has a value and a data type. The simplest expressions are literals and variables, and more complex expressions can be constructed from operands, operators and parentheses. An expression can itself be an operand in an expression. The syntax of this representation is

```
expression     = monadic.operator operand
               | operand dyadic.operator operand
               | conversion
               | operand
operand        = element
               | literal
               | table
               | (expression)
```

so an operand is either an element of a data type, a literal, a table or another expression enclosed in parentheses. Elements have already been considered in connection with array types.

We have already pointed out that all variables must be defined and associated with a single data type. All primitive types, apart from **CHAN** and **TIMER**, have the assignment operator defined. Literals, which are textual representations of a known value, can also be used with all data types.

Literals have not been presented before, and their syntax is

```
literal        = integer
               | byte
               | integer(type)
               | byte(type)
               | real(type)
               | string
               | TRUE | FALSE
```

```
integer      = digits | #hex.digits
byte         = 'character'
real         = digits.digits | digits.digitsEexponent
exponent     = +digits | -digits
digit        = 0 | 1 | 2 | 3 | 4 | 5 | 6 | 7 | 8 | 9
hex.digit    = digit | A | B | C | D | E | F
```

All characters are coded according to their ASCII code, so that the character a has a value of 97. A character enclosed in a pair of single quotes, such as 'B', is a byte value, unless its type is explicitly stated otherwise in parentheses after its value, as in the example below for K. A string literal is a sequence of characters enclosed in a pair of double quotes, such as "today" in the example below. Each component of the string is represented by the ASCII code for that particular character, so that "today" is represented by the values, 116, 111, 100, 97, 121. Some examples of literals are:

```
J := 6                an integer literal
Running := TRUE       a boolean literal
Char := 'b'           a byte literal
Mail := "today"       a string literal
Pi := 3.1416          a real literal
Inc := 0.3E+2         another real literal, value 30.0
Delta := 1.4E-2       yet another real literal, value 0.014
```

In order to clarify the type of a literal, its type may be added in parentheses after the literal, for example,

```
e := 2.718 (REAL32)
```

is valid. This can be extended in a useful way to provide a possibility to respecify the type of a literal. For example,

```
K := 'B' (INT)
```

means that the character literal which is of type **BYTE** can be interpreted as a value of another integer type.

To return to the nature of expressions, the following are all valid expressions:

```
2.718 (REAL32)        a literal value
x                     a variable
3 + 2                 addition of two literal operands
x - y                 subtraction of two variables operands
NOT FALSE             a boolean expression
```

An expression can itself form the operand in an expression, and by this means larger expressions can be built up, for example,

```
(x * y) + z              multiply the variable x and y and add
                         the variable z to the result
```

Unlike some other systems there is no operator precedence and the hierarchical structure of expressions has to be shown by the use of parentheses, as in the case above. It should also be noted that with the exception of shift operations, the data type of the two operands in a dyadic expression must be of the same type. In an assignment the value of the expression has to be of the same type as the variable to which it is to be assigned.

A table constructs an array of values, each component of which is the value of the corresponding expression, from a number of expressions. The values must be of the same type. The syntax for the table is

```
table           = table [subscript]
                | [{1,expression}]
                | [table FROM subscript   FOR count]
subscript       = expression
count           = expression
```

so that a table is one or more expressions of the same data type which are separated by commas and enclosed in square brackets. Line breaks are permitted after a comma. For example,

```
[a,b,c]             a table of three values
['d','o','g']    a table of three bytes equivalent to "dog"
```

One of the major uses of tables is in assigning values to arrays, for example:

```
[8]INT a.1, a.2:

INT i.1, i.2, i.3, i.4:
SEQ
   a.1 := [0,1,0,1,0,1,0,1]
   [a.2 FROM 0 FOR 4]  :=   [0,1,0,1]
   [i.1,i.2,i.3,i.4] := [a.1 FROM 3   FOR 4]
```

would all be valid assignment statements.

6.1 Arithmetic operators

As has already been described, operations evaluate operands and produce a result. For the case of arithmetic operations, the following operators exist:

```
+          addition
-          subtraction
```

*	multiplication
/	division
REM	remainder
\	remainder
PLUS	modulo addition
MINUS	modulo subtraction
TIMES	modulo multiplication
MOSTPOS	most positive
MOSTNEG	most negative

The operations of addition, subtraction, multiplication, division and remainder perform operations upon operands of the same integer or real data type, but not on boolean or byte data types. The result of an operation produces a result of the same data type as the operands. If the data type of the result is not compatible with the data types of the operands then the operation is invalid. For example if the multiplication of two integers exceeds the most positive integer value then the operation is invalid. Division by zero is also an invalid operation.

An expression is defined to be an operand followed by an operator followed by another operator. The operand itself may be either a variable or another expression. However, if the operand is another expression then it must be contained within parentheses, so that if we wish to evaluate an expression such as

```
A + B + C
```

then written in this form it is invalid. It can only be evaluated if written, in this case, as

```
(A + B) + C      or    A + (B + C)
```

It is clear then that this means there is no need to have a defined order of precedence.

Examples of the use of arithmetic operations are

```
48 + 6      gives result 54
48 - 6      gives result 42
3  * 4      gives result 12
12 / 3      gives result 4
14 REM 3    gives result 2
14 \ 3      gives result 2
```

As regards division, the use of **REM** and \ produce the same result, namely the remainder after division of the appropriate value. The sign of the remainder is the sign of the left-hand side of the expression regardless of the sign of the right-hand side. When the data types for the division are integers then the operation of / produces truncation of the result. In the above example of 12 / 3 the result would be 4 but if the values where 13 / 3 the result would still be 4. Notice that the result is truncated and not rounded.

The results of arithmetic operations on real numbers are rounded to the nearest value that can be represented by that data type. Some care must be taken when considering the effects of rounding on the results of division of real numbers. When using / with real data types the result is rounded towards zero, in contrast to truncation which results in the case of division by two integer types. It is possible for the result of a real remainder expression to be negative, for example

```
2.4(REAL32) REM  3.0(REAL32)
```

gives the result (–0.6). The rules for rounding that are used are those defined by ANSI/IEEE standard 754-1985. In this case, if we take a general expression of the above,

```
a REM b
```

where a and b are real numbers, then the result is defined by

```
(a - (b*n))
```

where n is given by dividing a by b and rounding towards zero. So, in the above example, n = 2.4 divided by 3.0 gives 0.8 which when rounded to the nearest integer gives the value 1. So the expression is then evaluated as

```
(2.4 - (3.0 * 1))   which equals  (-0.6)
```

The modulo arithmetic operations of **PLUS**, **MINUS** and **TIMES** perform operations on data items of the same integer data type. Operations on other data types of real, boolean and byte are invalid. The operations are similar in effect to the corresponding arithmetic operations already described. However, no overflow checking is performed on the operation and so the values are cyclic. Before illustrating this effect it is preferable to introduce the operations of **MOSTPOS** and **MOSTNEG**. **MOSTPOS** produces the most positive value of the integer data type, and **MOSTNEG** produces the most negative value of the integer type. The syntax for these operators is

```
expression    = MOSTPOS type
              | MOSTNEG type
```

where the keyword **MOSTPOS** or **MOSTNEG** appears to the left of the type. In the case here we have

```
MOSTPOS INT16        gives the value 32767
MOSTNEG INT16        gives the value -32768
```

Returning now to illustrate the differences between arithmetic and modulo arithmetic operations, we can consider

```
32767(INT16) + 1(INT16)        arithmetic overflow - invalid
32767(INT16) PLUS 1(INT16)        gives the value -32768
(-32768(INT16)) - 1(INT16)     arithmetic overflow - invalid
(-32768(INT16)) MINUS 1(INT16) gives the value 32767
10000(INT16) * 4(INT16)        arithmetic overflow - invalid
10000(INT16) TIMES 4(INT16)       gives the value -25535
```

It should be borne in mind that the **AFTER** statement for reading from timers looks at the unsigned value of an integer. As a result,

```
32767(INT16) PLUS 1(INT16)
```

is indeed, **AFTER**

```
32767(INT16)
```

despite the result of the addition being an apparently negative number.

6.2 Bit and shift operations

The bit pattern of values of the data type integer may operated on by bitwise operations. The possible operations are

```
/\              bitwise AND
\/              bitwise OR
><              bitwise exclusive OR
~               bitwise NOT
```

The result of a bitwise operation is of the same type as the operands. In some implementations where there is a reduced character set, keywords **BITAND, BITOR** and **BITNOT** are equivalent to /\, \/, and ~ respectively. The results of the corresponding operations are:

```
Bitwise AND     Bitwise OR    Bitwise exclusive OR Bitwise NOT

0 /\ 0 = 0      0 \/ 0 = 0        0 >< 0 = 0          ~0 = 1
0 /\ 1 = 0      0 \/ 1 = 1        0 >< 1 = 1          ~1 = 0
1 /\ 0 = 0      1 \/ 0 = 1        1 >< 0 = 1
1 /\ 1 = 1      1 \/ 1 = 1        1 >< 1 = 0
```

For example, if we take the following values, all of type INT16,

```
pattern1 #C3C3     i.e.      1100001111000011
```

```
pattern2 #9B9B    i.e.    1001101110011011
pattern3 #0404    i.e.    0000010000000100
pattern4 #FFFF    i.e.    1111111111111111
```

then for the following operations we have

```
pattern1 \/ pattern2    gives #DBDB    i.e.    1100001111000011
                                        OR      1001101110011011
                                                ----------------
                                        #DBDB   1101101111011011


pattern1 >< pattern2    gives #5858    i.e.    1100001111000011
                                        XOR     1001101110011011
                                                ----------------
                                        #5858   0101100001011000


pattern4 /\ pattern3    gives #0404    i.e.    1111111111111111
                                        AND     0000010000000100
                                                ----------------
                                        #0404   0000010000000100
```

This example of the AND function illustrates the ability to provide a mask to interrogate the setting of bits within a bit pattern:

```
pattern1                gives #3C3C    i.e.    1100001111000011
                                                ----------------
                                        NOT  #3C3C  0011110000111100
```

Whilst this gives the complement of the value, we could achieve the same result by use of the exclusive OR with the value #FF. For example,

```
pattern1 \/ pattern4    gives #3C3C    i.e.    1100001111000011
                                        XOR     1111111111111111
                                                ----------------
                                        #3C3C  0011110000111100
```

In addition to these bit operations, there are also operations which allow the shifting of values to left or right by a specified number of places. Shifts are only possible on values of data type integer, and the operation is given in the form

```
value << count    shift left by number of places in count
value >> count    shift right by number of places in count
```

The shift operation is not cyclic and there is no carry so that bits shifted out from the most significant bit on the shift left are lost, and zeros are added to the least significant bit on each shift. In the case of shift right, bits shifted out from the least significant bit are lost and zeros are added to the most significant bit on each shift. If the value is of type **INT16** and of value, called x say, #C39B, then we could have

```
x << 3              #C39B              1100001110011011
                    shift 3 places left 0001110011011000
```

giving #1CD8. For the case of

```
x >> 4              #C39B              1100001110011011
                    shift 4 places right 0000110000111001
```

the result is #0C39. If count is 16 then for integers of type **INT16** the result is zero whether the shift is to the left or right. Similar results occur if the integer type is **INT32**, only count would need to be 32 before the value was always zeroed. In cases where count > 16 for **INT16** or count > 32 for **INT32** integer types the shifts are invalid. Shifts are also invalid if count is specified as being negative.

One application for these bit operators is in picking areas out of input–output registers on physical devices. If an input–output device has a status register of size **INT16** where the top eight bits are a status value and the bottom eight bits are a device number, we could do the following:

```
INT16 register.value:
INT16 status.bits:
INT16 device.id:

SEQ
   register.value := Register
   status.bits := (Register AND #FF00) >> 8
   device.id := (Register AND #00FF)
```

If we want to construct a value to write into an input–output register, we could reverse the process:

```
INT16 register.value:
INT16 status.bits:
INT16 device.id:

SEQ
   -- assign device.id
   -- assign status.bits
   register.value := (status.bits << 8) OR device.id
```

6.3 Boolean operations

The boolean operators combine operands of the boolean type, and the possible operators are:

```
AND       boolean and
OR        boolean or
NOT       boolean not
```

The following results are then produced:

- **AND**

```
false AND true    =  false
false AND false   =  false
true AND false    =  false
true AND true     =  true
```

- **OR**

```
false OR false    = false
false OR true     = true
true OR false     = true
true OR true      = true
```

- **NOT**

```
NOT false         = true
NOT true          = false
```

During the evaluation, the operand to the left of the operator is evaluated. If the result of this evaluation and the nature of the operator is such that the result is then determined, then the evaluation stops at that point and the operator to the right of the operator is not evaluated. For example, for the expression

```
IF
    ch >= 'd' AND ch <= 'x'
```

then if the condition ch > = 'd' is false there is then no need to evaluate for the condition of ch < = 'x' since the outcome is false. If the expression is altered to

```
IF
    ch >= 'd' OR ch <= 'x'
```

then if the condition ch > = 'd' is true then there is no need to evaluate the condition of ch < = 'x' since the outcome is true.

6.4 Relational operations

The relational operators perform a comparison of the operands and produce a boolean result. The possible relational operators are

```
=    equal
<>   not equal
<    less than
>    greater than
<=   less than or equal
>=   greater than or equal
```

In the case of relational expressions which use the operators = and < > the operands may be of any primitive type. However for expressions which use any of the other operands, namely <, >, < =, > = then they may only be used in conjunction with operands which are of type integer, byte or real and may not be used with boolean operands. To illustrate the operation, consider the operands b and c to be of the appropriate type as required, then

```
b = c     is true if the value of the operand b is equal
          to the value of operand c otherwise the result is
          false
b <> c    is true if the value of the operand b is not
          equal to the value of operand c otherwise the
          result is false
b < c     is true if the value of the operand b is less
          than the value of operand c otherwise the result
          is false
b > c     is true if the value of the operand b is greater
          than the value of operand c otherwise the result
          is false
b <= c    is true if the value of the operand b is less
          than or equal to the value of operand c otherwise
          the result is false
b >= c    is true if the value of the operand b is greater
          than or equal to the value of operand c otherwise
          the   result is false.
```

Other operators can be combined with **BOOL** variables and operators to calculate quite complex conditions. For instance, to decide whether a character is a control character, as opposed to being out of range or a printable character,

```
BYTE ch:
BOOL is.control:

SEQ
  is.control := (ch < #FF(BYTE)) AND ((ch < ' ') OR
                (ch > '~'))
```

6.5 Other operations

In addition to the operations that have been described so far in this chapter, some other expressions exist which are worth noting. We introduce here two such expression operations, **AFTER** and **SIZE**. The expression **AFTER** has already been used in connection with the use of the **TIMER**. The operator **AFTER** performs a comparison and returns a boolean result to test whether one operand occurs after another. If b and c represent two operands then the expression

```
(b AFTER c)
```

will return the result true if the operation of b is in a later cyclic operation than that of c. Whilst this was introduced in the context of timing and the clock, it can be used for any types which are represented in a cyclic sequence. If the shortest route in such a sequence from the first operand to the second operand is clockwise then the result of the expression will be true, but if the shortest route from the first operand to the second is anticlockwise then the result will be returned as false. Thus for a cyclic series of operands the expressions of

```
(b AFTER c)
```

and

```
(a MINUS c) > 0
```

will produce the same result.

The operator **SIZE** has a single operand of array type and it produces an integer value of type **INT** which gives the number of elements in the particular array. For example if b is an array of type [16]INT, then

```
SIZE b
```

will produce the value of 16 as the result.

As an extension of this to a more complex array definition, if b is an array of type [16][8]INT, then

```
SIZE b      gives the result 16 as before
SIZE b[1]   gives the result 8
```

Once again bear in mind that arrays in occam are indexed from zero. This means that statements such as

```
[ ]INT a.1:
```

```
SEQ ix = 0 FOR SIZE a.1
    --- process
```

index from 0 to (**SIZE** a.1 – 1). This is quite confusing at first, but should be borne in mind.

6.6 Data type conversions

For logical shift expressions, the number of bits to shift must be of type **INT**, whereas for other expressions, the operands must be of the same type. It is possible for operands to have their type explicitly converted which allows a value of a primitive data type, and hence not an array type, to be converted to a numerically similar value of a different primitive data type. The syntax for the data conversion is given by

```
conversion   = primitive operand
             | primitive.type ROUND operand
             | primitive.type TRUNC operand
```

The data type, which appears to the left of the operand, must be a primitive data type. For the case of the data type conversion **ROUND** a value is produced which is rounded to the nearest value of the specified type. In the situation where the two values are nearly equal the value is rounded to the nearest even number. For example, consider the conversion of the following real numbers to integers.

```
INT32 ROUND 0.8(REAL32)       gives a value of 1
INT32 ROUND 0.2(REAL32)       gives a value of 0
```

If b and c are real numbers of value 5.5 and 4.5 respectively, then we obtain the following from the conversion to integers.

```
INT16 ROUND b        gives the value 6 rounded even
INT32 ROUND c        gives the value 4 rounded even
```

For the case of the data type conversion **TRUNC** a value is produced which is truncated to a value of the specified type, where truncation means rounded towards zero. For example the corresponding effect to the cases considered above would produce

```
INT32 TRUNC  0.8 (REAL32)       gives the value 0
INT32 TRUNC  0.2 (REAL32)       gives the value 0
```

Using the same values for the real numbers b and c gives

```
INT16 TRUNC  b                        gives the value 5
INT32 TRUNC  c                        gives the value 4
INT16 TRUNC  (b/c)                    gives the value 1
(INT ROUND b)  *  (INT ROUND c) gives the value 24
```

A conversion between any of the integer types, and conversions between those types and the type **BYTE** are valid only if the value that is produced is within the range of the receiving data type. In particular byte and integer types may be converted to each other if their value is one or zero. Thus,

```
BOOL 1                          gives TRUE
BOOL 0                          gives FALSE
INT TRUE                        gives the value 1
INT FALSE                       gives the value 0
```

7 Procedures and functions

7.1 Abbreviations

Before considering the use of procedures and functions in occam, we must introduce the use of abbreviations. There are two kinds of abbreviations, which can be used to specify

- a name for an expression
- a name for an element

The name which is specified in the abbreviation is then used as an alias for the expression or the element.

The syntax for the use of an abbreviation which specifies the name for an expression is

```
abbreviation  = VAL specifier name IS expression:
              | VAL name IS expression:
specifier     = primitive.type
              | []specifier
              | [expression]specifier
```

The abbreviation of a value starts with the keyword **VAL**. An optional specifier which specifies the data type of the abbreviation appears to the right of **VAL**, and this is followed by the keyword **IS**. The abbreviated expression appears to the right of the keyword **IS**. Continuation lines are allowed after the keyword **IS**. The data type of the expression must be of the same type as that of the specifier, which itself can usually be omitted from the abbreviation since its type can be inferred from the expression that is being abbreviated. A specifier [] type simply defines the abbreviation as being an array with components of the specified type. We have already met some of these concepts in section 4.1.3 when considering constants, for example,

```
VAL INT week IS 7:
```

could equally be written as

```
VAL week IS 7:
```

since the data type of the abbreviation week can be inferred from the fact that the constant 7 is of type **INT**. Here the name week is defined as an abbreviation constant value 7. For the following example

```
VAL INT weeks.in year IS 52:
```

specifies the name weeks.in.year for the constant value of 52. Again the use of the abbreviation has already been used in another example in section 4.1.3 where the constant value to be used to test for termination was given the name terminate:

```
VAL INT terminate IS (-1):
```

The abbreviated expression must be a valid expression, so that it must not overflow and all subscripts must be within range. Variables which are used in an abbreviated expression may not be assigned to by an input or assignment within the scope of the abbreviation, which is the region of a program where the name is valid. This means that the value of the abbreviation stays constant within the scope of the abbreviation. So, for example,

```
VAL REAL32 y IS (m * x) + c:
```

means that no assignment can be made to the parameters m, x or c within the scope of the abbreviation.

Abbreviations such as the name of an element may be made for an element of an existing variable, channel, timer or array. The syntax for the use of abbreviation as the name for an element is

```
abbreviation    =: specifier name IS element:
                |  name IS element :
specifier       =: primitive.type
                |  []specifier
                |  [expression]specifier
```

The abbreviation of an element begins with an optional specifier. The name specified appears to the right of the optional specifier followed by the keyword **IS**, to the right of which appears the abbreviated element. Continuation lines are allowed after the keyword **IS** or after any other valid point in the element. The type of the element must be the same as the specifier for the abbreviation to be valid. Just as with the abbreviation of expressions, the specifier can usually be omitted from the abbreviation since it can be inferred from the type of the element. A specifier []type defines an abbreviation as being an array with the components of the specified type.

As examples of abbreviation of an element,

```
INT b IS c:
```

would specify the name b as the new name for the element c, and

```
INT x IS a.1[1]
```

would specify the name x to the element of the array a.1 which is the second component of the array namely a.1[1].

As with the case of the abbreviation of expressions, care must be taken that when abbreviating components of an array, all the components of the array remain identified by a single name within any given scope. Checks are made to ensure that two abbreviations which identify segments from the same array do not overlap: this would then be invalid.

7.2 Scope

In the previous section we have considered more formally the use of abbreviations, though they have been used earlier in the book. We have also referred to the scope in connection with abbreviations. This concept is not itself new, but is worth summarising the formal syntax for scope as follows,

```
process         =: specification
                   process
choice          =: specification
                   choice
option          =: specification
                   option
alternative     =: specification
                   alternative
variant         =: specification
                   variant
valof           =: specification
                   valof
specification   =: declaration
                 | abbreviation
                 | definition
```

This syntax specifies the point in a program where a declaration, abbreviation or a definition may occur. The specification may appear before a process, choice, option, alternative, variant, or valof. The region in the program where such a specification is valid includes any other specification which may occur at the same level of indentation, and the corresponding process, choice, option, alternative, variant or valof. For example,

```
INT y:              -- integer variable y
SEQ                 -- scope
   input ? y        --
   ALT              --
```

```
REAL32 y: - real y hides integer variable y
chan ? y - scope
... - scope
```

Notice in this example that the apparent conflict in specification of the variable y is covered by the limits of the scope of each specification. Because of the change in level of indentation necessary within the **ALT** construct, the second declaration has the effect of hiding the earlier use of the same name y for the duration of its scope. All names within a given scope in occam are distinct. The association of a name with a particular scope can be either local, and as such specified at the start of the scope under consideration, or free of local association. If as in the example above a specification is made of an existing name, in that case y, then the new meaning supersedes the old meaning for the duration of the scope of the new specification. The above program could equally have been written as

```
INT y:              -- integer variable y
SEQ                   -- scope
   input ? y         --
   ALT               --
      REAL32 x:          -- real variable x
      chan ? x           -- scope
      ...                -- scope
```

7.3 Procedures

In occam the basic operation is that of a process. Procedures in occam provide a definition of a name for a process. For example, for the process below,

```
PROC decrement (INT y)
SEQ
   y := y - 1
:
```

gives the name 'decrement' to the occam process which performs the operations between the name and the terminating colon. In this case the process is simply the operation $y := y - 1$. The parameter y in the case above is a formal parameter of the process and is specified in parentheses after the procedure name. Having defined the procedure decrement then it may be subsequently used in a program; for example,

```
INT x:
SEQ
   ...
```

```
decrement (x)
  ...
```

The syntax for the definition of procedure is

```
definition     = PROC name ({0, formal})
                   procedure.body
                :
```

The keyword **PROC**, the name of the procedure, and a formal parameter list enclosed in parentheses is followed by a process which is indented by two spaces and is the body of the process. The procedure definition is terminated by a colon which appears on a new line at the same level of indentation as the start of the **PROC** definition.

The syntax of when the procedure is called from within the program is

```
instance  = name ({0, actual})
actual    = element
          | expression
```

The instance of the procedure is the name of the procedure followed by a list of zero or more actual parameters in parentheses. An actual parameter is itself either an element or an expression. The list of actual parameters must correspond directly to the list of formal parameters used in the definition of the procedure. The actual parameter list must have the same number of entries, each of which must be compatible with the kind and type of the corresponding formal parameter. It should be noted that unlike those in some other languages such as Pascal, occam procedures are not recursive. A channel parameter or free channel may only be used for input or output, but not both, in the procedure.

In section 7.1 we considered the definition for abbreviations. The rules for the parameters used in procedures are the same as those described for abbreviations. A name which is free within the body of the procedure is statically bound to the name used in the procedure definition.

One of the major uses for a procedure is to take a particular task, or section of a task, and define it separately. One example which has appeared several times above is the example of a filter process which takes data from a channel, looks for a particular value and outputs the remaining data on a channel.

Using the protocol definition

```
PROTOCOL Int.Or.Message
  CASE
    Dump.Count
    Int.Value; INT
:
```

we could define a procedure to achieve the filter process as follows:

- count the number of items of value 'val'
- when we get a 'Dump.Count' message output the count and terminate

```
PROC filter.value(INT val
                  CHAN OF Int.Or.Message input, output,
                  CHAN OF INT dump)

  BOOL running:
  INT local.value, count:

  SEQ
    running := TRUE
    count := 0
    WHILE running
      SEQ
        -- look for a data value or a Dump.Count message
        input ? CASE
          Int.Value; local.value
            IF
              local.value = val
                count := count + 1
              TRUE
                output ! local.value
          Dump.Count
            SEQ
              -- output the count and terminate
              PAR
                dump ! count
                output ! Dump.Count
              running := FALSE
:
```

We can use this procedure to form a pipeline of filter processes. Using procedures in this way makes it much simpler to modify a large pipeline, either to change the size or change the data values.

The above procedure could be embedded in a larger occam program in the following way, where we assume the same protocol definition:

```
-- define a list of data values to be looked for

VAL [5]INT values IS [1,3,5,7,9]:
```

```
-- define the channels connecting the filter processes

[SIZE values + 1]CHAN OF Int.Or.Message chan:

-- define the channels connecting the filtering processes to
the output

[SIZE values]CHAN OF INT dump.channels:
```

Notice that we define the channel arrays using '**SIZE** values' – this allows us to disregard the actual size of the 'values' array and write the program to work with any number of values. If we want to change the size of the pipeline, we simply change the contents of the 'values' array. This technique generalises quite nicely to pipelines in two dimensions, that is array or processes.

However we now have a problem – if we look at the pipeline, we realise that the final filter process has no channel on which to output. There are a number of solutions to this problem. One simple method is to create a 'dummy' process which sits at the end of the pipeline and consumes data items without doing any useful work. This procedure will look something like the following:

```
PROC consume(CHAN OF Int.Or.Message input)

BOOL running:
INT local.value

  SEQ
  running := TRUE
  WHILE running
    SEQ
      input ? CASE
        Int.Value; local.value
          SKIP
        Dump.Count
          running := FALSE
:
```

Taking this approach has the advantage of keeping the pipeline symmetrical. We can assume that we have a corresponding procedure called feeder to pass data into the pipeline.

So, the main program will look like the following:

```
PAR
  -- run the feeder process at the beginning of the
  -- pipeline
```

```
feeder(chan[0])
-- run the filter process in parallel
PAR ix = 0 FOR SIZE values
  filter.value(values[ix], chan[ix], chan[ix+1],
  dump.channels[ix])
-- run the consumer process at the end of the pipeline
consume(chan[SIZE values])
-- run the dumpprocess which listens for the filters
-- terminating
dump.values(dump.channels)
```

Notice that each filter process at position 'ix' in the pipeline inputs on channel 'ix' and outputs on channel 'ix + 1'.

This example raises two general points about occam processes which are formed into pipelines. Firstly, it is usually wise to draw a diagram of the process pipeline and label the various processes and channels; this makes it much simpler to convert the pipeline into an occam program, since you can constantly refer back to the diagram to avoid confusion. Secondly, always take account of the beginning and end of a pipeline; the processes that feed and empty pipelines are just as important as the processes that form the core of the pipeline. Careful design of the boundary processes can often simplify the design of the core processes, making them cleaner and more efficient. For example, out-of-range data should always be filtered out by the process which is feeding the pipeline; in this way, the core processes need never concern themselves with invalid data.

The dump.values procedure looks at a range of channels, expecting data on all of them. The procedure definition for this will be

```
PROC dump.values([]CHAN OF INT dump.channels)
-- dump the counts
  :
```

Notice that the size of the channel array is not specified — it can be determined inside the procedure using '**SIZE** dump.channels'. The most obvious way to code this procedure is with a replicated **ALT** over the channels, of the form

```
INT local.value:
BOOL running:
SEQ
  -- initialise
  WHILE running
    ALT ix = 0 FOR SIZE dump.channels
      dump.channels[ix] ? local.value
        -- output the count
```

This allows the data to arrive from the filter processes in a completely arbitrary order. However, this makes the termination condition difficult to code. If we examine the filter pipeline we notice that the counts will be arriving in a completely predetermined order — as the Dump.Count message flows through the pipeline, the various filter processes pass on their counts and terminate. As a result, the channels on which the counts arrive will be ready in sequence along the pipeline from dump.channels[0] upwards. This implies that we can code the dump.values procedure as follows:

```
INT local.value:
SEQ ix = 0 FOR SIZE dump.channels
    dump.channels[ix] ? local.value
    -- output the count
```

There is no fear of deadlock in this case. This has the added advantage that the termination condition is clear — once every filter process has passed on its count, the dump.values process can terminate.

7.4 Functions

In the previous section a reminder was given that the basic operation in occam is that of a process, and that procedures were named processes. Functions also exist in occam and these refer to a special class of process, namely that of a value process. The syntax for the function is

```
value.process   = valof
valof           = VALOF
                     process
                     RESULT expression.list
                  | specification
                    valof
operand         = (value.process
                  )
expression.list = (value.process
                  )
definition = {1, primitive type} FUNCTION name ({0,formal})
                 function.body
              :
function.body   = value.process
operand         = name ({0, expression})
expression.list = name ({0, expression})
```

```
definition = {1,primitive.type} FUNCTION name ({0,formal}) IS
              expression.list
           :
```

A value process consists of zero or more specifications which precede the keyword **VALOF**, and this is followed by a process which is indented by two spaces and the keyword **RESULT** which is at the same level of indentation as the process. The keyword **RESULT** is itself followed by an expression list which follows the keyword and is on the same line as the keyword **RESULT**; the expression list itself can be broken after a comma or at another valid point in the expression, as discussed earlier in the general context of continuation lines. An operand of an expression may consist of a left parenthesis, a value process followed by a right parenthesis. The structured parentheses which are equivalent to the left-hand and right-hand parentheses of a bracketed expression appear at the same level of indentation as each other. Therefore where the value process produces a single result, the upper bracket may be preceded by an operator, or the lower bracket may be followed by an operator. The heading of a function definition consists of the keyword **FUNCTION** which is preceded by the type (or types) of the result (or results) of the function. The name of the function and a formal parameter list enclosed by parentheses follows, on the same line, the keyword **FUNCTION**. The value process which forms the body of the function follows on the next line with an indentation of two spaces. The function definition is finally terminated with a colon which is on a new line at the same level of indentation as the start of the definition itself. As an alternative definition to that just described, a function definition may consist of the function heading as before followed by the keyword **IS**, an expression list, and a colon, on the same line. As discussed elsewhere, the line may be broken provided this is done after the keyword **IS**, a comma or another valid point in the expression. Finally, where a function is defined to have zero parameters it must be followed by empty parentheses; and where a number of parameters of the same type appear in the parameter list then a single specifier may be used to specify several names.

The named value process which is specified by the function produces a result which is of primitive data type, and notably not of array type, and the result may appear in expressions. Value processes may produce more than one result which may be assigned in a multiple assignment statement.

It is useful to bear in mind that the **VALOF** expression can be used in an occam program to return a value — it is not restricted to being used in functions. For example, it would be quite valid to write in an occam program

```
[10]REAL32 A:
...
i := REAL32 tmp:
```

```
VALOF
  SEQ
    tmp := REAL32 0.0
    SEQ ix = 0 FOR SIZE A
      tmp := tmp + A[ix]
  RESULT tmp
```

There are a number of restrictions on the kind of expression that can appear in the context of a **VALOF**:

- variables that are assigned to must be declared immediately prior to the **VALOF**, or within the body of the **VALOF**
- there must be no **PAR** constructs
- there must be no **ALT** constructs
- there must be no channel operations

Like procedures, functions are often used to 'mark off' sections of occam code which are going to be used frequently. However, unlike a procedure, a function returns a value, or a number of values, rather than having an effect on the environment of the process. For example, a function to calculate the average value in an array of values could be written as follows:

```
REAL32 FUNCTION average(VAL []REAL32 values)

  REAL32 sum:
  VALOF
    SEQ
      sum := REAL32 0.0
      SEQ ix = 0 FOR SIZE values
        sum := sum + values[ix]
    RESULT sum/(REAL32 ROUND SIZE values)
:
```

We can also make use of multiple assignments in occam to write functions like the following:

```
REAL32, REAL32 FUNCTION average.and.max(VAL []REAL32 values)

  REAL32 sum, max:
  VALOF
    SEQ
      sum := REAL32 0.0
      max := values[0]
      SEQ ix = 0 FOR SIZE values
        sum := sum + values[ix]
        IF
```

```
      values[ix] > max
        max := values[ix]
      TRUE
        SKIP
      RESULT sum/(REAL32 ROUND SIZE values), max
:
```

Whilst in this example the assignments have been made to two values of the same data type, namely that of **REAL32**, assignments can be made to different data types. In this case the assignments are made to values for average and maximum.

Appendix A Syntax summary

The syntax of occam 2 is summarised in this appendix using BNF (Backus-Naur Form) notation.

A.1 Processes

```
process             = SKIP | STOP | action | construction
SKIP    starts a process, performs no action and terminates
STOP    starts a process but never proceeds and never
        terminates.
action              = assignment | input | output
assignment          = variable := expression
input               = channel ? variable
output              = channel ! expression
assignment          = variable.list := expression.list
variable.list       = {1,variable}
expression.list     = {1,expression}
```

A.2 Constructs

```
construction        = sequence | parallel | conditional |
                      loop | alternation | selection
sequence            = SEQ
                        {process}
parallel            = PAR
                        {process}
```

```
conditional            = IF
                           {choice}

choice                 = guarded.choice | conditional

guarded.choice         = boolean
                           process

boolean                = expression

loop                   = WHILE boolean
                           process

alternation            = ALT
                           {alternative}

alternative            = guarded.alternative | alternation

guarded.alternative    = guard
                           process

guard                  = input | boolean & input | boolean & SKIP

selection              = CASE selector
                           {option}

option                 = {1,case.expression}
                           process
                       |    ELSE
                              process

selector               = expression

case.expression        = expression
```

A.3 Replicators

```
sequence               = SEQ replicator
                           process

parallel               = PAR replicator
                           process

conditional            = IF replicator
                           choice

alternation            = ALT replicator
                           alternative
```

replicator	= name = base **FOR** count
base	= expression
count	= expression

A.4 Types

type	= primitive.type | array.type
primitive.type	= **CHAN OF** protocol
	| **TIMER**
	| **BOOL**
	| **BYTE**
	| **INT**
	| **INT16**
	| **INT32**
	| **INT64**
	| **REAL32**
	| **REAL64**
array.type	= [expression]type

A.5 Literals

literal	= integer
	| byte
	| integer(type)
	| byte(type)
	| real(type)
	| string
	| **TRUE** | **FALSE**
integer	= digits | #hex.digits
byte	= 'character'
real	= digits.digits | digits.digitsEexponent
exponent	= +digits | -digits
digit	= 0 | 1 | 2 | 3 | 4 | 5 | 6 | 7 | 8 | 9
hex.digit	= digit | A | B | C | D | E | F
string	= array.type

A.6 Declaration

```
declaration            = type{1,name} :
```

A.7 Protocol

```
definition             = PROTOCOL name IS simple.protocol :
                       | PROTOCOL name IS sequential.protocol :
simple.protocol        = type
                       | primitive.type :: []type
input                  = channel ? input.item
input.item             = variable
                       | variable :: variable
output                 = channel ! output.item
output.item            = variable
                       | expression :: expression
variable               = element
protocol               = simple.protocol
sequential.protocol    = {1;simple protocol}
input                  = channel ? {1;input.item}
output                 = channel ! {1;output.item}
definition             = PROTOCOL name
                             CASE
                                {tagged.protocol}
                         :
tagged.protocol        = tag
                       | tag;sequential.protocol
tag                    = name
output                 = channel ! tag
                       | channel ! tag;{1;output.item}
case.input             = channel ? CASE
                             {variant}
channel                = element
variant                = tagged.list
```

```
                        process
                      | specification
                        variant

tagged.list           = tag
                      | tag;{1;input.item}

process               = case.input

input                 = channel ? CASE tagged.list
```

A.8 Timer

```
primitive.type        = TIMER

input                 = timer input
                      | delayed input

timer input           = timer ? variable

delayed input         = timer ? AFTER expression

timer                 = element
```

A.9 Expression

```
expression            = monadic.operator operand
                      | operand dyadic.operator operand
                      | conversion
                      | operand

operand               = element
                      | literal
                      | table
                      | (expression)

element               = element [subscript]
                      | [element FROM subscript FOR subscript]
                      | name

subscript             = expression

table                 = table [subscript]
                      | [{1,expression}]
                      | [table FROM subscript FOR count]

expression            = MOSTPOS type
```

```
                              | MOSTNEG type
conversion                    = primitive operand
                              | primitive.type ROUND operand
                              | primitive.type TRUNC operand
```

A.10 Abbreviation

```
abbreviation                  = specifier name IS element:
                              | name IS element :
                              | VAL specifier name IS expression:
                              | VAL name IS expression:
specifier                     = primitive.type
                              | []specifier
                              | [expression]specifier
```

A.11 Scope

```
process                       = specification
                                process
choice                        = specification
                                choice
option                        = specification
                                option
alternative                   = specification
                                alternative
variant                       = specification
                                variant
valof                         = specification
                                valof
specification                 = declaration
                              | abbreviation
                              | definition
```

A.12 Procedures

```
definition          = PROC name ({0, formal})
                          procedure.body
                      :

formal              = specifier{1,name}
                    | VAL specifier{1,name}

procedure.body      = process
instance            = name({0,actual})
actual              = element
                    | expression
```

A.13 Functions

```
value.process       = valof

valof               = VALOF
                         process
                         RESULT expression.list
                    | specification
                      valof

operand             = (value.process
                      )

expression.list     = (value.process
                      )

definition          = {1, primitive type} FUNCTION name
                      ({0,formal})
                         function.body
                      :

function.body       = value.process
operand             = name ({0, expression})
expression.list     = name ({0, expression})
definition          = {1,primitive.type} FUNCTION name
                      ({0,formal}) IS expression.list :
```

A.14 Configuration

parallel	= **PLACED PAR** {placement} | **PLACED PAR** replicator placement
placement	= **PROCESSOR** expression process
parallel	= **PRI PAR** {process} | **PRI PAR** replicator process
alternation	= **PRI ALT** {alternative} | **PRI ALT** replicator alternative
process	= allocation
allocation	= **PLACE** name **AT** expression:
definition	= specifier name **RETYPES** element: | **VAL** specifier name **RETYPES** expression:
primitive.type	= **PORT OF** type
input	= port ? variable
output	= port ! expression
port	= element
protocol	= **ANY**

Appendix B ASCII character codes

					Bit	Most significant hex digit							
						0	1	2	3	4	5	6	7
					b_7	0	0	0	0	0	0	0	0
					b_6	0	0	0	0	1	1	1	1
					b_5	0	0	1	1	0	0	1	1
					b_4	0	1	0	1	0	1	0	1
0	0	0	0	0		NULL	DLE	SPACE	0	@	P	'	p
1	0	0	0	1		SOH	DC1	!	1	A	Q	a	q
2	0	0	1	0		STX	DC2	"	2	B	R	b	r
3	0	0	1	1		ETX	DC3	#	3	C	S	c	s
4	0	1	0	0		EOT	DC4	$	4	D	T	d	t
5	0	1	0	1		ENQ	NAK	%	5	E	U	e	u
6	0	1	1	0		ACK	SYNC	&	6	F	V	f	v
7	0	1	1	1		BELL	ETB	'	7	G	W	g	w
8	1	0	0	0		BS	CNCL	(	8	H	X	h	x
9	1	0	0	1		HT	EM	)	9	I	Y	i	y
A	1	0	1	0		LF	SS	*	:	J	Z	j	z
B	1	0	1	1		VT	ESC	+	;	K	[	k	{
C	1	1	0	0		FF	FSR	,	<	L	\	l	|
D	1	1	0	1		CR	GSR	-	=	M	]	m	}
E	1	1	1	0		SO	RSR	.	>	N	↑	n	~
F	1	1	1	1		SI	USR	/	?	O	_	o	DEL

Least significant hex digit

Bit b_3 b_2 b_1 b_0

Appendix C Keywords in occam 2

AFTER   later than operator
ALT   alternation construct
AND   boolean operator AND
ANY   anarchic protocol
AT   at location
BITAND   bitwise operator AND
BITNOT   bitwise operator NOT
BITOR   bitwise operator OR
BOOL   boolean type
BYTE   byte type
CASE   case input, selection construct, variant protocol
CHAN OF   channel type
ELSE   default option selector
FALSE   boolean value
FOR   count
FROM   base value
FUNCTION   function definition
IF   conditional construct
IS   specification introduction
INT   integer type
INT16   16-bit integer type
INT32   32-bit integer type
INT64   64-bit integer type
MINUS   modulo subtraction operator, negative operator
MOSTNEG   most negative integer
MOSTPOS   most positive integer
NOT   boolean operator NOT
OR   boolean operator OR
PAR   parallel construct
PLACE   allocation
PLACED   placed processes
PLUS   modulo addition operator
PORT OF   port type

PRI priority construct
PROC procedure definition
PROCESSOR processor allocation
PROTOCOL protocol definition
REAL32 32-bit real type
REAL64 64-bit real type
REM remainder operator
RESULT value process result
RETYPES retyping conversion
ROUND rounding operator
SEQ sequence construct
SIZE array size operator
SKIP skip process
STOP stop process
TIMER timer type
TIMES modulo multiplication operator
TRUE boolean value
TRUNC truncation operator
VAL value
VALOF value process
WHILE loop construct

Bibliography

Barron, I. M. (1978) 'The Transputer', in *Microprocessor and Its Applications*, pp. 343–357. Cambridge University Press.

Ben-Ari, M. (1982) *Principles of Concurrent Programming*. Englewood Cliffs, NJ, Prentice-Hall.

Dijkstra, E. W. (1975) 'Co-operating sequential processes', in Genuys, F., *Programming Languages*. London, Academic Press.

Dijkstra, E. W. (1975) 'Guarded commands, nondeterminacy and formal derivation of programs'. *Communications of the Association for Computing Machinery* 18(8), pp. 453–457.

Hoare, C. A. R. (1978) 'Communicating sequential processes'. *Communications of the Association for Computing Machinery* 21(8), pp. 666–677.

Hoare, C. A. R. (1981) 'The emperor's new clothes' (1980 ACM Turing Award Lecture). *Communications of the Association for Computing Machinery* 24(2) pp. 75–83.

Hoare, C. A. R. (1985) *Communicating Sequential Processes*. Englewood Cliffs, NJ, Prentice-Hall.

Inmos Ltd (1984) *Occam Programming Manual*. London, Prentice-Hall.

Inmos Ltd (1987) *Occam 2 Product Definition (Preliminary)*. Bristol, INMOS.

Liskov, B. L. and Scheifler, R. (1982) 'Guardians and actions: linguistic support for robust, distributed programs'. *ACM Transactions on Programming Languages and Systems* 5(3), pp. 381–404.

May, D. and Shepherd, R. (1986) *Communicating Process Computers*. Bristol, Inmos.

Roscoe, A. W. and Hoare, C. A. R. (1986) *The Laws of Occam Programming*. Oxford University Programming Research Group, PRG-53.

Index